The Peanut Factory

a memoir

Deborah Price

Guts Publishing

Praise for *The Peanut Factory*

'Telling journal about the London squat scene in the post punk era. Compelling and disturbing in equal measure — especially the outside toilets.' — Jim Tavaré, comedian, actor and musician

'A window into a time of raw energy and rough edges, Deb Price paints a vivid picture of life in the squats of South London. By turns amusing and alarming, but always engaging, we accompany a teenager as she navigates her way to womanhood in a subculture on the margins.' — Allie Rogers, author of *Little Gold* and *Tale of a Tooth*

'An engaging memoir that describes accurately and with great warmth the squatting scene that provided housing for thousands of people and was an important part of the counter culture in the last quarter of the 20th century.' — Christian Wolmar, journalist and author of *Cathedrals of Steam*.

'A beautifully grungy coming-of-age memoir set in the squats of 1970s London. Deborah Price is a gifted storyteller who reminds readers how it feels to be young, broke, uncomfortable and marginalised, but gloriously hopeful and madly in love with life. A must-read for anyone who was there, or wishes they had been.' — Nikki Sheehan, author of *Goodnight, Boy*

'*The Peanut Factory* journeys deep into the squatland of 1970s Britain. Evocative and heart-wrenching by turn, this is a story from a time of possibility, when people like Deborah Price knew there was a world to win.' — Matt Worley, professor of Modern History, University of Reading

'Deborah Price's debut memoir paints a vivid and gritty picture of living in squats around south London in the late 1970s with tales of the harsh living conditions and the many characters she encountered. It's frank and candid which is just how it should be in telling a story that sometimes takes a few tragic turns. Croydon Punk/New Wave music fans will be pleased to hear that the South London band The Damned/Johnny Moped get a mention along with Captain Sensible AKA Ray Burns who she encountered at a local music festival. A great read and thoroughly recommended.' — Mark Williams, author of *Smash-It-Up*

In memory of
my mother Sheila Mathieson
my father Red Price
and my stepfather Monty Lubert.

The Peanut Factory

I left home on a summer morning in 1975. I was eighteen and ready for change. In the afternoon I went to a pop festival in South London. In the evening I moved into a squat with my boyfriend and partied all night. Music and parties and moving every few months would become my life for the next eight years. I had no idea what I was in for...

Chapter One

My stepfather shoved all of my things in the boot of the car. Not much. Clothes, books, a chest of drawers, and little things I treasured. My childhood books tumbled out, lying in the boot like abandoned orphans of an Edwardian institution: *The Secret Garden*, *A Little Princess*, *Five Children and It*.

In silence we drove to my new home, a big room in a Victorian squat. It was in Crystal Palace, a part I didn't know, just behind where the buses stopped and right by an estate of prefabs. Not far, about a twenty-minute drive. When we got there it was dark and only a few of the streetlights were working. The road was pockmarked with holes and bits of gravel. It had been raining as we drove and the gravel shone blue and black under our feet when we got out of the car.

'It's that one there,' I said pointing. I couldn't tell him this was the first time I had seen it. He looked up at the large building. I didn't know if he had taken in the decrepit air of the street and the run-down look of the house.

'I haven't got much time,' he said, his mouth screwed up with effort as he opened the boot. His body blocked mine as I stepped forward to help and his arms grabbed everything carelessly. He showed less thought getting everything out than when he was packing away his market stall. My life's possessions were not as important as ladies' tights, knives, and the roller thing that gets lint off clothes.

The larger furniture tumbled out first then my smaller things that he shoved onto the road. A crochet shawl fell into a rain puddle followed by my dress from Kensington Market. I heard a faint tinkle and saw a little wind chime in broken pieces. Something inside me clenched with regret. At that moment I was close to putting it all back in and going home.

'Is that OK? Is that everything?'

'Yes, I think so.'

'OK, I'll be off then.'

He didn't ask to come inside, and didn't help me take anything in. Stiffly, after all the bending, he walked round to the driver's side of the car. The light from the streetlamp caught his glasses. He paused and turned towards me. I stood in the minimal light, my bravado gone, clutching my broken wind chime and my shawl like they were precious friends.

'I'll be off then,' he repeated.

There was a pause and a nod, then he got into the car and did a complicated manouvre to turn round without driving over my things and drove away. I stood in the dark, the smell of London petrichor wafting from the surface, the hot evening drying the damp, watching his taillights get smaller and smaller.

'He wanted me gone anyway,' I thought.

I walked up the stairs to the front door and looked for a knocker. There was a bell, so I pressed it and heard the sound echo inside the house. No one came so I tapped on the door. Still no one came, and I was worried, looking at my pile of possessions at the kerb and wondering if another car would come and run over them.

'Hallo,' I called up, my voice unsure and thready.

The street was silent like it disapproved of me being there.

2

Every atom of it was unfamiliar and strange. I felt like the air was repelling me and telling me I wasn't wanted. I tapped again and called, 'It's me.' A window went up on the middle floor and a head came out.

'Oh, aye it's you. I forgot you were coming. Hold on a minute, hen.'

It was Jimmy, the Scottish boy I had met, and the best friend of my boyfriend. I had met him before Joe when he started coming into the pub where I worked. He was charming and funny and I really fancied him but then I found out he had a girlfriend. I think he felt the same towards me but was loyal to Jill and encouraged Joe to make a play for me to keep me close.

Jimmy had told me they were opening up a new squat. I had asked shyly if they had a room free and he said, 'Well, aren't you moving in with Joe?

'He didn't ask me,' I said feeling stupid.

'Oh, aye he's into it. He told me before he went away.'

And this was me now standing outside having made the sudden decision to come that evening. I felt like a house of cards that was about to come tumbling down. I was eighteen and had just finished my A levels that summer. Home felt strange. My mother had gone to America to work and I had spent my whole life battling my stepfather so it felt alien to be in the house just with him, the non-parent, and my little brother. To him I wasn't a child; he had never fathered me, but I wasn't an adult either. It was too difficult and weird to work, so I wanted out.

I hadn't seen Joe for over a week. He had only come back from Germany that evening. Maybe he wasn't 'into it' like Jimmy said.

Despite the cool evening, sweat prickled under my arms. My eyes felt hot and my throat got narrow and lumpy. I steeled myself; whatever happened I mustn't cry like a baby. I was an adult now and about to start a new and exciting life. Only it didn't feel new and exciting. I suddenly felt a wave of regret for my home that I had carelessly discarded like an old newspaper. I fancied sitting in the living room, even though it was a Saturday night. Sitting in the living room drinking a cup of tea and watching 'High Chaparral' with my stepfather on the flickering screen of the big cabinet in the corner. 'Hey Manolito,' he would say in a fake Spanish accent when that character came on screen. Our silence would be something approaching companionable.

The front door creaked. I blinked in the light pouring out into the street, swallowing tears. I tried a smile and Jimmy bounded out followed by Joe who wrapped me in a bear hug. They both looked behind me at my pile of gear.

'This yours then?' Joe said. 'You moving in?'

'Course she is,' Jimmy said as he started to scoop up my possessions.

'We'll have this all in in no time and then we're going out,' he said.

'Going out?' I said.

'It's Saturday night and we're off to a party in the prefabs.'

Joe started picking things up and moving them inside. 'We're up on the first floor,' he said. 'The kitchen's on the top floor and some junkies have moved in but I think they're OK.'

At the top of the step he turned and looked at me, his head poking out from behind my shoes, skirts, and books. 'By the way, first rule of squatting, never ring the bell. Only pigs and bailiffs ring the bell. Just knock and eventually someone will come. And if you're inside and you hear the bell, never answer it. If you hear a knock, open the window to check who it is before you answer the door.'

I nodded and couldn't believe that I had broken some sort

4

of basic rule before I had even set foot in the house.

My new family took all of my things from the street and piled them in the middle of the room. Jimmy left us and went next door where he started moving things around and sneezing.

'It's bigger than I thought it would be,' I said kicking the clouds of dust and wondering if it would be laughable to ask for a broom. It smelt of damp and emptiness. Joe lit a joss stick and wedged it between the sash window frame.

'We'll make it look nice,' he said putting his arms round me. Looking at the high ceilings, I wondered about curtains. There was a door to the next room, but Joe had blocked it off by putting a mattress there for us to sleep on. It looked a bit stained, but I had an Indian throw that would cover it. I could see that my chest of drawers would look perfect in one corner and started to cheer up. We kissed.

'What's this about a party?' I said.

Joe sat on the mattress and shrugged. 'There's one over the road if you fancy it.'

I tried to comb the tangles out of my hair with my fingers. I didn't want to stay in this room with him, not yet. 'Yeah, sounds great,' I said and leant against the wall, avoiding the mattress and trying to summon up enthusiasm.

Joe stood up and cracked his knuckles. 'OK let's split then. We can sort this lot out tomorrow,' he said then knocked on the adjoining wall and shouted, 'Party!'

The party was across the road in a prefab. The one-bedroom bungalow seemed homely and sweet after the echoing spaces of our Edwardian house. I danced and drank, felt adventurous and adult. I had left the confines of childhood and was with my tribe, launched on the world.

The next day I grieved for the broken windchimes and felt bereft at the way I had left home.

For those first two weeks in the squat I hardly ate. Food tasted like ashes in my mouth. I had the odd bit of toast. I had a continual unreal feeling as I went about my daily life. It reminded me of when I was at school and we had to close our eyes to pray in assembly. As soon as we did that I would sway to keep my balance. That's what I was doing now, swaying continuously as I tried to make this new life balance.

I managed to get up and get dressed for work. The boys all wore the same kind of clothes: tatty jeans and ratty Shetland wool jumpers with the elbows poking out. Joe was more adventurous and sometimes wore pale blue cord dungarees with long flowing scarves. He was good looking and closely resembled Patti Smith on the cover of *Horses* — a fact he was well aware of and played up to. He liked a feminine look and I sometimes came home from work to find him pottering around in one of my skirts with a beret on.

My boyfriend showed me how to make a basic tomato sauce that we could add to pasta. I wondered who had shown him, how he knew these skills. He could cook, sew, make things out of rescued rubbish from skips, and turn electricity on illegally.

All I could do was go out to work.

Chapter Two

The landlord of The Queen's Arms did a lot of huffing and puffing when he interviewed me. 'We'll give you a try and see how you go,' he said, in reality eyeing me up and pulling on his handlebar moustache. 'Alright, darling?'

His wife could barely keep her grip on the barstool. Swaying and drinking Jameson's, she whispered to me, 'It's for me nerves, love.' Occasionally she lurched off and tottered up the steps to the ladies followed by her Alsatian, a vicious mutt who slavishly protected her. Bar staff and regulars knew to give it a wide berth and especially keep away from her handbag. It was very proprietorial about that black battered bag, and rumour was that the landlord had to pay damages to a girl the dog had bit after she picked it up from the floor thinking it was hers.

It was an Irish pub with music and entertainment including 'The fabulous Eammon Baxter' who would play his guitar and sing rousing rebel songs during 'lock ins'. Being able to stay for a lock in was a mark of being a true regular and sadly none of my crowd made it, too broke and too rowdy. I hated being asked to stay as it meant working until the early hours and then walking home on my own.

After a week I was left in charge of the upstairs bar. Under the eagle eye of a regular who would report back if I was nicking, I stood and polished glasses dutifully. Eventually I was trusted to be on my own so Joe and my friends came in and perched on the bar stools in front of me with hopeful looks.

'You're so stingy,' Joe said. 'I thought having a girlfriend who worked in a pub would get me free drinks.' He was teasing but I took him at his word.

'Right. You want free drinks, I'll give you free drinks, but you've got to drink right along this row of optics, one from every one and then the bottles at the back.'

'Even Campari?'

'Even Advocaat,' I said. They staggered out at closing time looking green around the gills. I wasn't asked about free drinks again.

Every evening when I wasn't working, we went to a pub. Busman's holiday for me, but I got to know all of the locals.

'What about The Crown?' I said.

'Nah,' Jimmy said. 'That's a copper's pub.'

'What about that one,' I said and pointed to The Alma.

'Nope, we don't go there,' Joe said.

'Why not?'

'No idea,' he shrugged. 'We just don't.'

I looked inside The Cambridge but one glimpse of the rough looking clientele had me backing out. 'Don't fancy it, hen?' Jimmy said. 'I don't blame you. That's where you go when you're barred from everywhere else.'

'Tell you what,' Joe said. 'Let's go to The Swan. They've done it up and the strippers are only on at lunchtime.'

'What about all those Angels?' Jimmy said.

'Oh, don't worry about them,' I said. 'They'll leave you alone if you're with chicks.'

We strode into the pub and saw that the brewery had decided to go upmarket and get rid of the greasy rocker clientele

8

and reputation. Pale pink velvet banquettes were installed and it reopened with an art deco 1920s vibe. It didn't work though. The motorcycle gangs just came in and put their boots all over the velvet and soon it looked like the shithole it had always been.

Inevitably most nights we ended up in The Queen's Arms, just the other side of the bar for me. At closing time there would be a shout of, 'Drink up, we're off,' from Joe. Everyone would down their pints and get up.

'Where are we off to?'

'Over the road.'

The Queen's Arms was in Croydon and closed at 10:30pm, so we all crossed the road then for an extra half an hour of drinking in a Lambeth pub.

One morning in my daytime job I had bad news. 'I'm sorry love but you can't work at two pubs. I'm going to have to let you go,' said the landlord of the Crystal Palace Hotel, Mr Ford. It wasn't a hotel but a big London pub with a barn-like structure off the back that was a disco in the evenings.

I'd already been 'let go' at The Railway Tavern, a Young's real ale pub off Gipsy Hill, my first job after A levels. They said I was too slow. I wasn't too slow for the CPH. I worked day times and it was deathly quiet. There was just a smattering of regulars nursing a pint and sometimes a ploughman's lunch. I was so bored with my quiet days, and I needed extra money, so I started working evenings at The Queen's Arms and I had been grassed up.

'I don't understand why?' I pleaded. 'I can be here in the day and there in the evenings. You don't need me in the evenings and The Queen's Arms don't seem to mind. They know I work here as well.'

'Well, I'm sorry but that's how it is. We're a jealous lot us publicans and I don't want The Queen's Arms to know all of our business. You have to stay loyal to one pub. You can work until the end of the week and I'll see about a little bonus because you're a good girl but I can't do any more.'

The whole thing seemed ridiculous and part of some secret landlord's code that only Mr Ford adhered to. I was relieved not to be in the quiet old man's pub anymore and to have an excuse to leave. The bonus came in handy as well.

So I was now working daytimes and some evenings at The Queen's Arms. They needed me for the famous 10p a pint Mondays. It was on these Mondays that I originally got to know Joe and Jimmy. All the hippies and wastrels came in that night because it was so cheap. Johnny Rotten was a regular and various other n'er do wells and squatters. The landlord and his wife disapproved of them all, but I was in heaven.

Our squat was just past The White Swan, past the parade of shops and the bus terminus, first left down the hill. It attracted residents quickly. Living on the ground floor was the sweetest couple, Rosy and Gerry, who always seemed like they'd come up from a rural idyll and not at all like London hippies, no edge to them at all. They lived in domestic bliss with their own front door, painted purple with a peace sign in white, their own kitchen and toilet, and a little mutt called Ringo. The first time I went there I made a great fuss of him and his whole body wiggled with joy. But when I got up to go, he uttered a low threatening growl and showed his teeth. Gerry lunged at him to save me. 'He doesn't like anyone going,' Gerry explained. 'He attacks them.'

Rosy and Gerry had come from Joe and Jimmy's previous squat. I'd been there a couple of times when I first started seeing Joe and was living at home. It was an abandoned newspaper office in the middle of Crystal Palace in St Aubyn's Road, but they hadn't been there long before getting evicted hence the move to Farquhar.

On the ground floor were three big bedrooms. Tom, another Scot, occupied one. 'But I can never go back there,' he often said, shaking his head sadly.

He had some kind of awful scar that he once showed Joe.

'I never want to see that again, bloody awful,' he said. Joe and Jimmy weren't that keen on Tom, but he's the one who had found and initially broken into Farquhar Road so he got first pick of the rooms. Next to him were two guys who occasionally worked on building sites, drinking buddies of Tom's and seemed OK.

Upstairs Joe and me had one room and Jimmy and his girlfriend, Jill, had the other. An internal door linked the rooms and the bathroom was next to us. Upstairs, the top floor had a tiny kitchen and two small attic rooms. One was empty initially, and in the other lived two junkies, Lucy and Robin.

I was nervous to meet them. My preconception of junkies was an image of cadaverous mumbling spectres. In fact, both of them were functioning addicts and fine as long as they had their fix. I first encountered Lucy in the wee small hours as I crept up to the kitchen to make a cup of tea.

'Hello, darling,' she said, standing up from the oven door and moving aside to let me in the galley space.

'Oh hi, I'm Deb from downstairs. I'm just making a cup of tea.'

'Oh, I really fancied a roast lunch,' she said waving vaguely at the mess in the kitchen. I didn't want to mention that it was 2am. As Lucy was fussing in the kitchen, I waited for the kettle to boil and took the opportunity to have a good look at her. She was pretty in a very English rose peaches and cream way, older than me, and posh. Her clipped voice suggested a private school.

'Do feel free to use my china but be careful with it — it's Portmeirion, you know.' As she stirred some gravy, I had to admit that the smells coming from the oven were lovely and the glimpse of the roast potatoes made my mouth water.

A man came out of their room. 'Juicy Lucy, where's my grub?' he said. Now this was more my idea of a junkie. Long greasy stringy hair, stick thin and a nasally whiny voice.

'Oh, Robin wait a minute. I've got to put the greens on.'

'I don't need the greens. Dish it up.'

'Now Robin, you know it's important to have your daily vitamins. We have to have greens to keep ourselves healthy.'

Robin ignored me and I felt a bit embarrassed to be around their bickering. I decided to forget the tea. 'Well, bye then,' I said a bit lamely and went downstairs. I couldn't wait to tell Joe the whole story.

'Loose Lucy we call her,' he said. 'I think she might be on the game?'

'But what about the Portmeirion and the roast dinner and the accent?'

'Oh yes when she's together she's quite the grand lady but that's not often.'

Joe was right. The whole time I was in the squat I never saw her again. Robin sometimes came whinging round us trying to bum fags and money. The only thing I ever saw him eat was lemon and lime Angel Delight, which they had quite a few packets of stashed away in a drawer.

Bang Bang Bang.

The second morning loud knocking on the door woke me at 8am. 'What the fuck,' Joe said, turning over and trying to get

12

back to sleep. I heard Jimmy get up, then his door opened and he ran downstairs.

'Get up, Joe, something's happening,' I said and went over to the window. Pulling aside the fabric we had hung there, I saw a crowd of about five men outside looking up and scowling. I ducked down and said, 'Joe, get up. Jimmy needs you.'

Complaining, Joe got up and struggled into his jeans. At the window he muttered something under his breath, then went downstairs. I hoped the other blokes would be there as well.

'Deborah, Deborah!' someone called and I poked my head out the door.

'What?'

'Come down, we need a chick.'

I threw my nightie on and pattered downstairs. All the blokes were clustered round the front door looking wide-eyed.

'Hello,' Jimmy shouted through the door.

'Open up,' came the reply.

'Who are you?' Joe said.

'Never you mind that, just open up.'

'Not until you tell us,' Jimmy shouted.

I heard him giggling and there was something quite funny about the whole situation. I felt a little hysterical myself.

Pushing my way to the front I said, 'If we open the door will you tell us who you are?'

Following a stunned silence, one voice said, 'They've got a woman there.'

'OK, just open up.'

Joe nodded at Jimmy and they slowly opened the door.

Clustered on the front steps were five middle-aged men who looked like ordinary middle-aged blokes, like my stepfather but a bit taller. Because of the steps they were lower than us so we had an advantage. The building site guys were muscly and fairly imposing. Jimmy and Joe were tall but lankier. All of the boys were bare chested and crowded round behind me. I could smell sweat from the night and the sharp scent of adrenaline. I shivered in the morning air in my nightie and a crocheted shawl I had grabbed on the way down. Joe put his arm round me. We seemed to be the self-elected spokespeople.

'We don't want any trouble,' Joe said.

One man in the front stuck out his chin and said, 'We just want to know what you're doing here.'

'What's it to you man?' Jimmy said, leaning forward in challenge.

Joe stopped him with a hand gesture and said in a level voice, 'We're just living here. Living here like you lot are.' (He told me later that he recognised some of the men from the adjoining houses and realised they were neighbours.)

'Well, it's not your house,' shouted one of them.

'Maybe not,' Joe said. 'But we're here now legally. We've changed the locks and we're paying our rates and leccy.'

'You're making too much noise,' one in the back row replied.

The rest of the guys behind us moved backwards. Tom was scratching his hair and yawning. He could sense there was no immediate threat and seemed bored with the exchange. I could feel the heightened mood dissipating.

'I got to get to work,' Tom said.

'Sorry about that, folks,' Jimmy said. 'We'll try to keep it down. Is there anything else?'

The deputation muttered among themselves then in a deflated tone their leader said, 'We just didn't know what was going on.'

'Well, we're just living here,' Joe said. 'And I need to get my breakfast and a cup of tea now.'

He moved back and made as if to shut the door but in a last ditch attempt the neighbour put his foot in there and said, 'Well just make sure you're quiet or we'll get the police round.'

Joe smiled and waited until he removed his foot before he shut the door. Then we collapsed against it, muffling our laughter until we heard them go down the steps and down the street.

'And that, my dear, is the end of that,' Jimmy said dusting his hands.

'What's going on?' Jill said, stood at the top of the stairs in her nightie peering through her hair.

'Oh, Jimmy and Joe just saw off a pack of neighbors,' I said.

They both bowed. Then the other guys reappeared and there was a lot of laughing and manly slapping on the back.

We all crowded upstairs into the little kitchen and had cups of tea, spilling onto the hall outside.

'It always happens,' Joe said and blew the steam off his tea. 'They always come round to check us out.'

'They can't do anything though,' Jill said, leaning against the bannisters.

'They can eventually,' Jimmy said. 'This is a council property so it would take them a long time, but if they tried hard enough and we made a nuisance of ourselves they could get us evicted.'

Joe struck a pose and said, 'We'd never let them pass.' Throwing a hand into the air he said, 'We'd be the Farquhar martyrs. We'd make barricades of mattresses and put tables on their sides. They'd never get through and we would never ever leave.' Then he struck his hand onto the cooker for emphasis.

'Yes, we would man,' Jimmy said. 'We'd just leave and find somewhere else.'

The house next door had been turned into flats. I never worked out if they were squats or not. A sweet little tabby cat had made its way into our building and seemed to want to adopt us. She was young but independent and made it clear that we were her new owners. I felt that we should try to find out where she came from before we took her in, so I went door knocking.

A young lad opened the first door I rang on and said, 'Yes, she's mine.' He was very young, with curly hair and still had puppy fat.

'Do you want her back?'

'No, I don't think she's happy here. I've got a few animals and she doesn't get on with them. Do you want to come in?'

A few animals was an understatement. Ryan was fifteen and had been chucked out of home. He had a dreadful family life, low self-esteem, and pets and assorted critters were his only friends. He had several Alsatian dogs (one very fierce that I was always scared of) and a parrot in a cage called Skip who was quite good at mimicking 'God bless you.' He would also scream and then start coughing, very realistically. There were some other cats and an assortment of caged gerbils, rabbits, and other small beasts.

He was like a hippy Gerald Durrell. Even by squat standards, his hygiene and housekeeping were lacking. It was always a bit nerve wracking going into his place as you never knew what would bite you or what you would step in.

'What's that Ryan?' I said, looking into a bucket.

'It's a few eels.'

I shuddered when I saw them all writhing and moving around.

Ryan was a sweet soul and genuinely devoted to his menagerie, so we took him under our wings. He became a feature of our lives and later moved with us when we left. We named the little cat 'Big Puss' which was either an appalling lack of imagination or might have been a protest against cute animal names.

Our house family was settling in. I liked living in the room next to Jimmy and Jill. The junkies upstairs kept themselves to themselves and Rosy and Gerry were always popping in and out. Rosy was a great baker and often came round for a cup of tea, offering a plate of fresh scones. The boys downstairs were mainly out at work. Having the little cat made the place seem like home. I felt safe and secure, like I could live there for years, but things were about to change.

Chapter Three

Gene was recently down from 'up the road', a shorthand term for Scotland and usually meant Glasgow. He was a small bloke, wiry, with curly hair and sharp blue eyes that never seemed to miss a trick. Wearing a checked shirt with the sleeves rolled up, I noticed some crude tattoos on his forearms. He always seemed to be moving, either jiggling his foot or clicking his fingers. His eyes had been following me round the room, so I escaped into the kitchen to make tea with Rosy.

I had no idea who had bought him round to the late-night drinking party that often happened after the pubs closed at 11. I asked Rosy and she pursed her lips. Drying a mug on a tea towel, she said, 'I think he came with that lot from the prefabs, or Joe started chatting to him in the pub. I think he's from the same area of Glasgow as Jimmy and Tom.'

'I just hadn't seen him before, that's all.'

'Don't ask him too many questions. I've heard he's some kind of hard man up there, probably on the run.'

She took some milk out of the fridge and sniffed it then handed it to me for a second opinion. I shrugged and started pouring it into the row of chipped mugs full of dark brown brew.

'Rumour has it he killed someone and that's why he's done a runner.'

'That's all we need, some kind of Scottish Kray twin.'

I heard an uproarious laugh from the other room, then Gene's pronounced Glasgow accent. He was holding court, and, by the sound of it, being entertaining. Everyone seemed to like him.

Rosy shrugged and said, 'The thing with squatting is it's free housing, that means free to everyone. We can't always choose who we live with and who comes round. We have to make sure that everyone has a bed for the night, isn't it?'

Slightly alarmed, I thought of the spare room on the top floor next to Lucy and Robin.

'At the moment,' Rosy said, putting the cups on an old, dented metal tray with a picture of a cottage on it. 'Gerry and me feel really lucky because we like all of you lot. We feel safe here, like a family. It hasn't always been like that.'

We took the tray next door where the party showed no sign of winding down. My heart sank. I was one of the few who had paid work and had to be up in the morning. Joe beckoned me over to sit on the floor next to him. We leaned against the sofa where Jill sat with Ringo, stroking his little pink nose. Jimmy had gone to Glasgow to see his parents for a few days. Gene sat opposite me on a chair. He raised his mug to me, winked and said, 'Cheers, hen.'

Joe put his arm round me. I could see from the brightness of his eyes and the way he kept licking his lips that he'd been taking speed. I knew he would probably stay up all night. That went for most of the others as well. A joint was going round and I passed it on without smoking.

'Do you indulge?' Gene said.

'Nope, she's a clean-living girl,' Joe said.

This was a slight bone of contention between us, and a source of bewilderment to our friends. I had smoked pot and dropped acid when I was younger, 14 – 16 years old. Then I went to sixth form college I stopped and didn't drink alcohol either. I had started drinking again, part of working in a pub, but didn't do anything else.

A ripple of disbelieving laughter passed round the group.

Gene leant forward and said, 'I'll give you a wicked blow back.'

I had had enough. I peeled myself to my feet and nudged Joe with my toe. 'I'm going to bed,' I said, with no expectation that he would want to come.

'OK, babe, see you later,' he said and barely looked up.

Jill smiled at me as I passed her. 'I'll be up soon,' she said. 'This new stuff Gene's got is a bit strong.'

That explained his popularity.

I went up to our room, got undressed, put my nightie on, and got in bed. I left a little bedside light on and lay on the mattress, covers tucked under my chin. We had made the room look nice with our collected bits of furniture and Indian throws on the windows as curtains. In the glow of the lamp it looked homely. There was a little sink in the corner which meant we didn't have to always venture to the grotty shared bathroom. A massive paper globe lampshade hung over the mattress. Joe was always knocking it down when he got into bed. There were bare boards and a slight smell of damp that we disguised with joss sticks. The room was slowly becoming familiar, and I no longer spent the first few minutes in the morning wondering where I was.

I read for a bit, a library copy of Daphne Du Maurier's *Rebecca*. The hardback kept banging against my nose as I dosed off, so I gave up waiting for Joe, turned the light off and settled myself in.

I woke suddenly with a sense that something wasn't quite right. I reached out a leg and Joe wasn't there so I knew it wasn't him who had disturbed me. The room was dark except for a crack of hall light from under the door. Someone was sitting on the floor in front of the door. They were silent.

Because I was half asleep I wondered if I was still dreaming, and hoped I was. I sat up in bed and said, 'Who are you?' My voice came out in a croak and I felt hot with fear.

'It's just me, just Gene, pet. I came up to see if you were alright?'

I sat up. I could see him now and I knew who it was. His curly hair was haloed by the glow from the hall but I couldn't see his face. Sitting cross-legged and hugging his knees, he was blocking the door.

'I'm fine,' I said, trying to keep my voice steady.

'I wondered if you wanted some company.'

'No, I want you to go.'

'There's no need to be like that. I'm just being friendly.'

'Joe will be up in a minute.'

'No, he won't. He's stuck into a session downstairs.'

'OK, well, I need to go to sleep now. I've got work in the morning.'

I wanted to sound calm and reasonable, in charge. That seemed to strike a chord. He stood up in a fluid motion, not a big man, but wiry.

'Oh well, I'll be off then, hen.'

He paused and looked at me. I held my breath, but he turned sideways and pulled the door open a crack, then edged out and closed it quietly. I heard his footsteps on the wooden floorboards as he went downstairs.

After he left, I took deep breaths trying to still my racing heart. I could've gone downstairs to get Joe, but I might have made myself look like an idiot. Gene hadn't actually done anything or threatened me. I couldn't see anyone down there taking it seriously, especially as they were all out of it. I blocked the door with some books and wished Ringo was there with me. I lay there on my side, knees drawn up, staring at the light under the door until I finally went back to sleep. Joe fell over the books when he stumbled in at dawn.

I woke at about nine and heard a strange snuffling noise. I nudged Joe but he was out for the count. Tottering into the hallway, bleary-eyed and hair sticking out, I discovered the noise was coming from Jill and Jimmy's room. I scratched softly on the door. No one answered but the noise continued, like muffled sobs. I pushed the door open and found Jill in a tangled heap on the bed. Wrapped in a nest of blankets and sheets, it was hard to find her. I sat on the edge of the bed and patted what I thought was her head.

'What's the matter Jill, missing Jimmy?'

The sobs intensified. There was a heartbreaking quality to them that worried me. She had seemed quiet since Jimmy had left, but he'd be back in a few days and she had us next door. We were new friends though. I hadn't known her long and felt a little out of my depth. I also knew I had to get ready for work.

'I'll go and see Joe,' I said brightly and slunk out.

Joe had been friends with her for longer and would know what to do. I went back to our room and shook him awake. He was good in a crisis.

'Joe, wake up, Jill's really upset.'

He blinked and rolled over, looking at me unseeing for a minute, lost in whatever dream he was having. Then he sat up and said, 'What's going on?'

'I don't know. She's all wrapped up in her bed and won't speak to me. She's really crying. I thought it was because she

22

missed Jimmy, but she's really really crying. Did anything happen last night after I'd gone?'

Joe scrambled to his feet and put on some jeans. He scratched his head and said, 'No, she went up before me. She seemed OK then, just a little out of it after that strong blow.'

'Well, go and check her out. I've got to get ready for work. I'll see you later.'

He went next door and I heard his deep voice and then just the sobbing noise again. I had a hasty wash in the sink and got dressed. If I were late to the pub, I'd get a telling off from the other barmaid, a fierce older woman called Rose. I'd hear all about it later. Maybe I'd get Jill some chocolate or a cake on the way home to cheer her up. I didn't know that I wouldn't ever see her again.

In the late afternoon I came home with a large bar of fruit and nut, her favourite. I called out but no one replied. Joe wasn't in our room upstairs. I knocked on the next door and said, 'Hello, Jill, you there?'

Silence. I turned the doorknob and cautiously went in. It was empty, but more than 'just nipped out for some fags' empty. Jill had strung some rope across an alcove to hang her clothes and that was bare. Her bookshelf was bare too and the rest of the room seemed different as well. The mattress where I had seen her huddled and weeping was still the same, blankets and sheets in a tangle. I squatted down and straightened them, smoothed the mess into order, wondering what was going on.

Floorboards creaked and I went back to my room. Joe was sitting on the mattress, looking tired. I sat down next to him.

'What's going on? Where's Jill?' I said and lit a cigarette then gave him one.

'I've just seen her off at Victoria Coach Station. She's off to see Jimmy.'

He inhaled and flicked the ash into an old cup on the floor.

'That's sudden. He'll be back soon. Is that why she was upset, she misses him?'

'No, it's not that. It's Gene.'

For once Joe seemed lost for words. He picked at the fringe on the bedspread and kept tapping the ash of his fag, flicking it into a cold cup of tea.

'How is he involved?' I said and remembered I hadn't had a chance to tell him what had happened to me. I started to feel cold.

'He raped her,' Joe blurted out and looked me right in the eyes. He was ashen.

'What?'

A panicky feeling came over me. This wasn't happening. Joe wasn't saying these words. I slumped against the wall and Joe held my hand, as much for his own support as for mine. He was shaking.

'It took me a while to get any sense out of her as she was crying so much.'

He took a deep breath.

'She told me that she was really out of it after that strong dope and went to bed and passed out. When she woke up he was in the bed, with a knife.'

Another deep breath.

'He held it to her throat and said that he'd cut her if she cried out.'

I made an inarticulate noise, and Joe's grip on my hand tightened.

'She said it was quick and afterwards he tried to go to sleep with her and wanted to cuddle. He wanted to pretend that he was her boyfriend or something.'

I shuddered and said, 'I thought she had a lock on her door?'

'Oh, it was just a little hook and eye thing to stop the wind blowing it open. He must've just pushed that out of the wall.'

'She managed to get him out of the room by saying that she heard me coming up the stairs and didn't want anyone to know about them because of Jimmy.'

'Christ.'

'I know. She said she just knew that she should play along. She told him that she liked him and that she'd see him later.'

I let out a moan and said, 'Oh fuck.'

Joe patted me and nodded.

'She was desperate and would have said anything to keep that knife away from her. After he'd gone, she pushed a chair under the doorknob and stayed awake all night.'

'Why didn't she come and wake us up?'

'She told me that she felt stupid for not fighting him. That she thought everyone would think she'd wanted him to do that. That he was so popular people would think she was just playing away from home while Jimmy was away.'

'Oh, for fuck's sake, poor Jill. That's awful. We wouldn't think that. I wouldn't think that.'

I stared at Joe. He raised his shoulders and dropped them.

'Of course, I wouldn't think that. She's a good friend of mine, her and Jimmy. Whatever she said I would believe.'

There was something obvious that I knew I had to say.

'What about the police?'

Joe looked at me like I was mad.

'Jill didn't want to involve them. She didn't know if they would believe her and didn't think they would ever catch him. She was worried the pigs would just take it as an opportunity to search the squat and bust everyone for whatever they could.'

I was going to protest but thought that he had a point. An American bloke had squashed my friend and me in a phone box once, wanked over us and then ran off. We went to the old Bill, but they just laughed and said that we deserved what we got walking around dressed like that.

'So, she's gone?'

'Yes, she phoned Jimmy and he told her to just come up there. They're going to leave Glasgow and go to Germany. He's got some mates who can put them up for a bit.'

'Has she taken all her stuff?'

'Everything she wanted. She told me if we wanted anything that was left to help ourselves. I helped her carry it all to the coach and loaded her on. Jimmy will meet her at the other end. She'll be OK. I gave her a mandy to relax her on the journey. I expect she'll sleep all the way there.'

'What about the room? I don't want anyone new in there, not with that door that leads into here.'

Everything suddenly felt unsafe. I shuddered and moved closer to Joe.

'Oh, don't worry about that, babe. We can have their room as our bedroom and this one as a living room.'

I wasn't sure if that was the answer either or if I would ever sleep easily in that room. There was another obvious question.

'What about Gene?'

Joe looked uncomfortable and shifted about on the bed. He rolled a cigarette and lit it. I flipped open my box of Benson and Hedges, took one out, and he held my shaking hand and lit my fag. We both inhaled and then sat in silence.

'I don't know,' Joe said.

I didn't want Gene in the house, and I wanted revenge, but I also knew about his hard man reputation, which had been born out by the rape and the knife. I didn't want Joe to confront him and get hurt.

'Where is he?' I said.

'I think he's over in the prefabs with the Scottish dealer, John.'

I knew who he meant. There was something unsavory about John, and on the rare occasions I had visited their place I felt sorry for his washed-out girlfriend who seemed to permanently be lying on their mattress smoking joints draped in scarves and shawls, a kind of South London Stevie Nicks. I avoided them both whenever I could.

'Tom knows them all.'

'Well, find out from him where Gene is.'

I finally told Joe what had happened to me. I know that if I had been in a stupor and hadn't heard Gene come into the room then it would have been me instead of Jill. Joe was horrified. He got up and started pacing around, running his fingers through his hair.

'Do you think we should split as well? Go somewhere else?' he said.

The thought was tempting, but I had a job and was just settling into my new life.

'Just find out what's going on.'

Joe left the room and I stayed on the bed, chain smoking and trying to read my book. It was impossible to focus, my nerve ends were twanging, and my foot wouldn't stop tapping on the floor. I slouched half on the mattress and half off, ready to spring into action if I needed to. In my head I was making lists, what I would do about my job, what I would pack, what I would tell my mum, stepfather, and brother, where we would go.

Just for something to do I went upstairs and made some toast and tea. I nibbled some and left the rest for Joe. I had put some cheese on it, and it lay there looking sweaty and unappetizing. I considered going downstairs to tell Rosy and Gerry what had happened just in case Gene was wandering around. I couldn't decide and seemed unable to move out of the room. I felt scared that I would run into Gene if I left the safety of my four walls. I knew I was being ridiculous, but I couldn't control my fear.

The house seemed quiet and I wondered where everyone was. I kept straining to hear something, but it was a big house and the walls were thick. I opened the door a crack and listened. I wondered if I heard voices downstairs, but I wasn't sure. I closed it again and the night carried on. I was continually getting up and down, peering out the window in the direction of the prefabs. I put some music on my portable turntable but it meant I couldn't hear anything else, so I turned it off and just carried on waiting. Sitting on the mattress shaking and smoking, watching the coils of smoke rise.

Around midnight the front door slammed. I heard Joe's steps coming from the ground floor and ran downstairs and found him. I could see that, for us at least, things were going to be OK. He looked relieved and colour had come back to his face.

'Gene's split, it's OK,' he said.

We went back to our room, sat down and we both ate the toast, suddenly hungry, then lit cigarettes.

'John the dealer is downstairs with Tom selling him some speed. I waited for ages in his place and he was here all along. He said Gene got back to his in the early hours this morning and was sobbing in a corner.'

'What?'

'That's right. He was crying and telling John that he'd done something bad, but he didn't know what.'

'Fuck me, what a psycho.'

'I know. John freaked out because, you know, the story is that Gene's on the run after killing someone up the road. If he'd done it again down here the last thing John wanted was the pigs all over him.'

'Oh, no thought for the person who Gene might've topped? Typical.'

'Anyway, the upshot is that John found someone who's driving back up the road today, and he talked Gene into going with him. He said the heat will have died down in Glasgow and that Gene didn't want new problems here. I think Gene was in such a state that he would've agreed to anything.'

'But Jill and Jimmy are up there.'

'Oh, they'll be gone by the time Gene gets there, and what's he going to do? He doesn't know Jimmy and I doubt if he'll recognise Jill again. I didn't tell John about Jill, I'm not sure why, but I don't trust the man and the last thing I wanted was for that news to be all over Glasgow. It's better if they choose who they tell.'

I was quiet. It didn't seem right that Gene was going to get off scot free for the things he had done. I was relieved though that the whole situation had moved away from our doorstep and up to Glasgow.

Joe started moving round the room. He put on some music.

'Jill said she'd write when they got somewhere and let us know where they were.'

'You'll miss Jimmy.'

'I know. He's my best mate. We've been through so much together. We opened the last squat and this one. He's such a nice bloke. I'm sure our paths will cross again though.'

'And Gene?'

Joe squatted and held both my hands in his.

'Don't you worry about him. Karma will get him eventually. And while we're waiting for that to happen, I'm going to put a big lock on both these doors.'

Chapter Four

The rape had really upset me. Every time I thought of how it could have been me, I felt cold and shaky. When I closed my eyes at night, I kept seeing Gene sitting by the door. In my dreams he was next to me and I could feel the cold steel at my throat.

Joe dragged our mattress next door into Jill and Jimmy's old room so we didn't have the empty room next to us but that only made it worse. Now I was sleeping where it happened instead of lying awake imaging it happening next door. On the surface everything should have been OK. Gene had gone, and Jill and Jimmy had moved onto the Isle of Wight where Jill was from. I didn't know if I would ever see them again and it was like they had never been there. Everything seemed to be back to normal, but I didn't feel that.

I went to the phone box at the top of the road. Phone boxes played a big part in my life. At home we rarely had a phone as it was always getting cut off because the bill wasn't paid. I spent a lot of time in the phone box across the road phoning 'Dial a Disc' to listen to pop songs or spend as much time as I had money gossiping to my friends. In a strange way the stagnant smell of copper money and wee that seemed to permeate all phone boxes was familiar and reassuring.

I dialed my mum. I didn't want to tell her what happened but wanted the familiarity of her voice.

'Hello, love how are you?'

'Oh, I'm OK.'

'Anything new?'

'No, I just wondered how you all were.'

'Oh, not too bad. Monty was a silly bugger, he rode your brother's chopper bike and a post office van came round the corner and he fell off.'

'Oh blimey, is he OK?'

'Yes, a cut on his head—' she carried on and I settled into the corner of the phone box feeding coins in until I had no more, smiling at the stories.

'I've got to go now, Mum, see you soon.'

'Alri—' the pips cut her off.

I felt better, calmer, and over the days things did go back to normal. Joe decided to go and see Jill and Jimmy in the Isle of Wight. He left for a week and I was tense at first because I kept thinking I would bump into Gene at any moment.

'He's gone,' Gerry said, with authority. I sat and petted Ringo and wanted to believe him.

'You won't see him again,' Rosy said, cutting me a slice of cake. They both sounded so sure that I let myself relax. The thought of never seeing Gene again was wonderful.

I managed to phone Joe once when he was away. In the phone box, Joe sounded tinny and far away: 'Jimmy agrees, they had their ears open in Glasgow but if he did come back then he's gone to ground. They're settled here, staying with Jill's folks for now, and send their love.'

'Send it back.'

I was learning that in squat life people came and went. Jimmy and Jill had been an integral part of my life for a while

32

but now they had gone, and I doubted if I would see either of them again.

'Oy oy,' Bobby said, coming round the corner into the kitchen while I was making a cup of tea. I worked with him in the pub but at home I had been quietly trying to avoid him. He settled onto the one stool.

'So, your man's buggered off and left you then?'

I squeezed my teabag and lobbed it at the bin where it left a trail of brown down one side. Staring at my milky tea, I said, 'He's only gone to the Isle of Wight for a week or so.'

Bobby clicked his tongue against his teeth.

'That's bad, hen, leaving you all on your own after what happened.'

The news had travelled fast round the house.

I leaned against the table and sipped my tea.

'I'm not on my own, it's only downstairs. I've got the blokes on the ground floor, Rosy and Gerry in the basement, and you lot upstairs.'

He stood up and squeezed past me to the kettle.

'Och well, those two junkies aren't much help. Yer men are out all the time and the basement two just have that wee idiot dog.'

He hunched over and spooned endless sugar into his mug. Then he straightened up and said, 'There's no other way. You'll have to come and stop with us while he's gone.'

'Fuck's sake, Bobby, how many are there in your room already?'

He made a big show of counting on his fingers.

'There's me and herself, the wee one, and my sister, Shona.'

'Well, one more won't fit into that small room. Besides you've left off the dog.'

33

'Oh, she's just a little dog, doesn't take up any room.'

'What about her puppies?'

'They're even smaller.'

I knew that by sheer force of will if I didn't stand up to him I would find myself crammed in there, engulfed by human and doggy concern and love.

'Bobby, you've got a double bed for you and Shirley, a single mattress for Shona, and a dog bed. Where would I fit?'

'You can top to tail with Shona.'

'She won't want my feet kicking her. She's pregnant, Bobby.'

* * *

Bobby drove me mad, but I loved him. He was like a big exuberant puppy, full of life and happiness. He was also a married man. It was a proper storybook tale of romance and excitement. I think he met Shirley when they were both sixteen and their respective families were on holiday in a Butlins somewhere. They kept in touch afterwards, in the face of much familial opposition on both sides, and then ran away to Gretna Green and got married. I was charmed by their story and by them. He was inevitably from the same Glasgow council estate as all the other Scottish men who were now in my life; and she was from a large and vociferous East End family who had initially taken great exception to the baby of the family being, as they saw it, kidnapped and forcibly married by an outsider.

Much negotiation ensued and eventually both families struck an uneasy truce. Bobby and Shirley were now a year older and Bobby was working as a potman in the Crystal Palace Hotel (the pub I had worked at in the daytime before going full-time at The Queen's Arms). He used to do the cruelest impressions

34

of the landlord and reduced me to hysterical laughter most of the day. The landlord of the pub, Mr Ford, showed his distaste constantly and obviously felt that he was destined for better, more cultured things than the grim environs that he now managed: a pub with two huge bleak bars, red split plastic couchettes all around the walls, and a cavernous disco in a hall behind it.

Mr Ford openly despised the motley assortment of regulars who gathered outside, ready to file in on the dot of 10:30am and kicked out at 2pm. They were a fairly rag tag crowd, I have to admit. Mostly elderly, barely functioning alcoholics who propped themselves up on barstools and nursed glasses of ale that we pulled with old fashioned hand pumps. Retired servicemen from the war with undisclosed injuries accompanied by their watery-eyed wives with felted winter coats, no matter what the weather, and thick American tan tights.

Mrs Ford was a small whispery blond whose main aim in life was to buy cheese and bread for the ploughman's lunches as cheaply as possible. Otherwise she just crept around the bar and barely said a word, in awe of her husband with his booming voice. The main barmaid, Janet, was a stern older woman with a strict moral code. She once told me that she wore nothing in bed but once a week hung a nightie out on the line so the neighbours wouldn't know.

Mr Ford and Janet knew that I had just finished my A levels and had decided not to go to university. They both deeply disapproved of me 'throwing my life away.'

'Ah the university of life — what a waste,' he would say looking soulfully at me.

It was deathly boring in the pub, and the only entertainment was Bobby. His job was to change the barrels in the cellar, keep it clean, oversee deliveries, and 'bottle up' which meant keeping

35

the shelves in the bar stocked. It was while doing that he would entertain me, and himself. He referred to Mr Ford as 'that one with the cravat' and lampooned him endlessly while squatting on the floor refilling tonics and juices.

'Oh, here they are, South London's finest. Ready to discuss Dickens and Bach,' Mr Ford would say as the doors opened in the morning. I would catch Bobby's eye and stifle giggles. He looked like a young Robert Mitchum with ink black hair and rolling blue eyes. We were the youngest people working there and became fast friends. I heard his whole life story.

'Bobby, how come there are so many Scottish blokes down here?' I said, polishing glasses and holding them up to the lights for smears. Loading the shelves with Britvic fruit juice bottles, he rocked back on his heels and said, 'Obviously I came down for love, hen. But I'm not sure about all those others. There's no work up the road now with all the shipyards closing. Nothing to do but go on the dole and hang around. See, we all think it's paved with gold down here and all you London lot just ponce about in tuxedos drinking champagne all day.'

He sighed and went back to work shaking his head. I looked round at the motley crew supping their pints. The sun coming through the window just highlighted the depressing bar with its Formica covered tables and lino floors. I sighed as well and flicked a fly away with my tea towel. 'It's not all it's cracked up to be living in swinging London, Bobby.'

After a discussion with Joe, I offered Shirley and Bobby the little attic room upstairs next to the junkies. At that time I hadn't met Shirley, and Bobby had neglected to tell me she was pregnant. She was a small, sweet-natured, plump young woman, always laughing at Bobby's jokes. With her pregnancy she grew as round as a little partridge. We had nothing in common, but I was fond of her. The night she had her baby Celtic were playing

36

Rangers and Bobby came back from the hospital desperate to hear the result. I had no interest in football but had been instructed by him to find out what happened as he rushed off to hospital.

Late that night he came back and rushed up the wooden stairs to find me making tea. 'What happened, who won?' he said, like a force of nature shouting from the landing.

'Never mind that, Bobby, what have you had? Boy or girl? How's Shirley?'

He refused to answer, demanding to know the football results. Exasperated I said, 'Oh for fuck's sake Celtic won, you nutter.'

He threw back his head and roared.

'Celtic won and it's a BOY!' he shouted, rattling the windows and waking everyone up.

He brought Shirley and baby Rob back to the room, then added to their brood with one of Ryan's puppies, which also swiftly got pregnant. Then one morning I found a tall young woman with long ebony hair and a floral nightie hanging round the kitchen and found out she was Bobby's sister, Shona.

'Are you just down for a visit then?' I said.

'Well...' she said and at that moment Bobby popped his head out of the room and told me the whole story. She had run away from her protective family and followed her big brother to London. There her initiative had deserted her and she mainly hung around the room helping Shirley with the baby and staring at the procession of hippies and druggies who filed in and out of the kitchen.

She was shy and I never heard her say more than a couple of words, to me or anyone else. But somehow when Bobby was working and Shirley was visiting her family Tom managed to persuade her to go over to the prefabs to a party. There she took speed for the first time, had sex with one of the dealers, and got pregnant.

Chapter Five

Joe came home from the Isle of Wight. He reported that Jill and Jimmy were doing fine and getting ready to hitch round Europe for the summer and maybe pick grapes in Crete in the autumn. The whole episode with Jill had unsettled us and the house didn't feel the same. Not like the welcoming home that it had been. We started using the abandoned room as a bedroom as well as the linked adjoining living room. With two interconnecting rooms all to ourselves there was plenty of space, but sharing the small galley kitchen with everyone was a pain. Especially with Bobby's expanding brood next door who treated it like an extension of their crowded room.

After hearing about Jill and Jimmy's travel plans, Joe felt restless. He wanted a new adventure and so found an empty house just off Gypsy Hill that he thought we could squat. It wasn't a council property like Farquhar, but we'd soon find out who owned it when we moved in and then see if we could do a deal with them.

We had been at our present house for about six months and could have stayed longer but it also felt OK to move. The building site guys downstairs had moved on and I was nervous about new tenants. There was an unspoken agreement that Tom could choose who moved into the downstairs empty room and I knew that he was mates with the dealers in the prefabs. The thought of another Gene moving in chilled me.

To my shame, I never took much part in opening up the squats and tended to leave that to Joe. He would go up to the electric shop on the high street and open an account for the property under an assumed name — most recently Neil Young and Graham Parker. We never paid the bills. The only bill we did pay was the rates, as non-payment would lead to certain eviction. None of the houses I lived in had heating or hot running water, some didn't have bathrooms and conditions were always a bit spartan. However, living with friends rent-free made up for that.

The day we moved to Camden Hill Road Joe took a load of speed to power through it. We loaded up a supermarket trolley and used it to take all our stuff in shifts. There was a shortcut through an alley to our new place and to move our mattress Joe just put it on his back and hurtled down the alley screaming the whole way.

We took Ryan and his animals with us when we moved. He had been getting grief from the neighbours because of his myriad creatures, and we had a soft spot for him. He had some intriguing stuff going on in his life. His family was a rock hard South London gang who had chucked him out of home. He was still on good terms with some of them, including a frightening sounding matriarch, his grandmother, who we heard hair-raising tales about. He was also unexpectedly good friends with Vivienne Westwood — I never found out how — and occasionally wore her clothes but inevitably his animals ruined them.

The new house was a shell, but a clean, bright, and damp-free shell. It was less crumbling than Farquhar Road and smaller. The basement had its own toilet but no kitchen. That had access to the garden, so we put Ryan there. Upstairs was a large room that Joe and I commandeered. It was next to the kitchen and the bathroom was one flight up. As usual there was no heat or hot running water but summer was approaching and it didn't feel like a problem. Another attraction was a flat roof accessed by a window off the stairs. Joe had his eye on that as a rooftop garden. Above us were three more bedrooms and a tiny attic room at the very top.

I was feeling more confident now and wanted a say in who lived in the house.

'I want another woman otherwise it's like a boy's club,' I said, angling to move my best friend in, Tessa. We had been mates since I was eight and this was our first opportunity to live together. I was so excited. She was living in a rented room in a shared house and was keen to move in with us. I met her in the local Wimpy and treated us to a knickerbocker glory.

'Who else is living there?' Tessa wanted to know.

'Ryan, animal boy, is in the basement. Me and Joe on the ground floor. Joe's mate Andy, and a bloke called Nick that Andy knows. He's upstairs. And a room for you. I've not met Nick yet.'

'What's Andy like?'

'Oh, you'll love him. He's an old mate of Joe's, a complete maniac. Wears suits and skinny ties all the time and is in a band. He's got short sticky-up hair and a strange moustache.'

'Not for me then.'

We both giggled.

The strange combination of people in the new house seemed to work. Tessa was like everyone's naughty big sister. She liked being with all the boys and constantly teased them. It was lovely having her in the house.

Andy was a ball of energy, sizzling and crackling with new ideas. He was always up for going out, listening to music, and talking into the early hours. It was great having someone in the house who liked to discuss music, politics, and books. Joe had known him for a while, so they had an established friendship that helped break the ice in the early days. Nick was quiet and soft-spoken but had a good sense of humour and already knew Andy — again it helped make connections in the house.

Joe and I were a bit like the mum and dad. It wasn't a role I particularly wanted to take on, but we were the common link for everyone. Also, Joe had opened the squat so that meant we had the main say in what went on in the house.

Ryan was down in the basement, a law unto himself. He liked being part of a gang though and quickly started to think of us as family. The kitchen was a hub of activity. There always seemed to be someone in there cooking, making tea, hanging out, and chatting.

Compared to the last house, there was a lot more music in this one. Someone always had something on loud. Andy was in a band and obsessive about punk and new wave. I told him the whole story of the festivals I'd organised. The one when I was seventeen and the one that happened the day I left home last summer.

The first year it went OK. I just had to pay for insurance and some little things. I found a great sound guy who did it all for free. We didn't have a stage and not many people came but it was great fun. For the second one, I wanted to do it bigger with more bands and a proper stage and more help. I persuaded an ice cream van to come, and my mum's friend sold sandwiches. Neither of them made much money but it was a sunny day and we had a good crowd. More than the previous year but hardly hordes.

I'd been to a free festival in Merton organised by the student union and it looked like fun so I thought I'd have a go myself. I found a great venue in a park, almost a natural amphitheatre, and contacted the council for permission.

As Andy and I sat and drank tea, listening to one of his new LPs, I told him about my mum and aunty selling sarnies at the festival. They were also selling cans of Peardrax, a horrible sweet soft drink that my stepfather was convinced was going to be the next big thing. 'Watch out Coca Cola,' he said when he lugged trays of it into the house. Mum looked flushed and warm at the end of the day and said, 'Not exactly Woodstock, is it darling? Still, we all had a good time. Apart from that godawful racket at the end.'

'That godawful racket,' I said to Andy, 'was The Damned. They'd played at the first festival and used another name, Johnny Moped. The sound guy had fallen out with them massively. "Never again," he said pointing his finger and pausing between each word for emphasis. "Never again will I have anything to do with that bunch of badly behaved nutters."'

For the second event, a year later, I agreed to book two friends' bands. Mates of Joe's with a rocky jive ensemble playing covers, and my college friends who called themselves Hairy Balls and the Masturbators. I met with the sound engineer to tell him and he said, 'I have a great band for the end. I haven't seen them but I've heard they're really amazing and they're looking for gigs. They're called The Damned.'

Halfway through the festival he stormed up to me and shouted, 'I told you I didn't want anything to do with those bastards!' Joe was just back from Germany and told him to cool it and passed him a spliff. I was bewildered. I hadn't booked them.

Then we saw Ray from Johnny Moped. He'd cut his hair short and ditched the velvet blazer from last year. His leather jacket had The Damned in white paint on the back. I turned to the sound guy and said, 'They've changed their name from last year, you berk. It's the same guys from the Mopeds.' He glared and stormed off muttering.

I announced The Damned over the PA to resounding silence. The crowd wasn't prepared for the music that followed. I wasn't sure that I was. Thrashing guitars and drums that didn't care if they were on or off the beat and a singer who shouted at the crowd as if he hated them.

I told Andy the whole story. Then I pulled out The Damned's first single 'New Rose' and got it out of the cover and played it to him. He was wildly enthusiastic and impressed with my taste. I think before that afternoon he had thought I was a bit staid.

'This changes everything, music won't be the same again ever,' Andy said. 'All of that Eagles, Doobie Brothers, ELP crap is gone now. Music belongs to the people and we can all form bands. Like I have. Like you and Joe and Tessa have. The Damned are incredible, do you want to play it again? This is the first punk single that's been released — it's amazing!'

Me: 'OK, but I'm not sure. It's a bit chaotic and I can't dance to it.'

Andy: 'Fuck dancing.'

He put it on again and jumped up and down, the floorboards creaking in protest.

I loved the concept but struggled with the sound of this new music until Andy took me aside some months later. It all seemed so raw and discordant. I'd only heard that one record, but I couldn't make sense of it and it didn't touch anything inside of me.

'Listen to this, I think I've cracked it with you. It's just been released, it's punk moved on a bit.'

It was 'Less than Zero' by Elvis Costello. I played it over and over again until the record wore out. I got the same feeling with the Sex Pistols. When I first heard 'Anarchy in the UK' I wanted to cry. It sounded like a rallying call. It was finally music that was part of my life, part of the London squatting scene.

I agreed with Andy. The old era was gone, long live the new. I got rid of all the vinyl that I decreed was irrelevant. I remember spending hours looking at the cover of *Who's Next* by The Who. I knew that I would never meet them, that their lives were so different from mine. I didn't have to think that with The Damned. I had met them and I knew what their lives were like. It was what my life was like. I just kept a few vinyl favorites secretly hidden away. Joe had got me away from glam rock and into the more American and Canadian mellow sounds of Joni Mitchell, Kate and Anna McGarrigle, Steely Dann, Hall and Oates. I was able to give them up in public but one thing I felt strongly about was that no one was going to put Motown down. That was the holy grail of music as far as I was concerned. Otherwise, I bought cassette tapes and played them on a tinny machine — Sex Pistols and Iggy Pop mainly.

A month after moving in it was inevitable that Joe would say, 'Let's form a band.'

It was the age of punk and we saw it as the end of the dominance of overblown rock gods. 'Those rich bastards, Led Zeppelin, The Stones. They've had it. Your band is the future,' Andy would say as he cranked up The Sex Pistols.

'I'm too old for punk. I'm nineteen. That's for sixteen-year-olds,' I complained.

'Oh, come on. We can be different from them.'

'OK, but no spitting.'

We called ourselves Johnny and the Lilets and sang acapella doo-wop in our living room. We never had any public performances but enjoyed ourselves. I sang backup vocals with Tessa and Joe cavorted around at the front.

'Dancing Tuesdays' was a regular event in the house. After everyone got back from the pub, we would pin up the long crochet lampshade in our room, put the music on, open the takeaway cans and dance around using Andy's superior sound system.

'Look at pixie girl,' Joe said, nodding his head in the direction of a small young woman dancing near the record player. She was crouched over with her hands on her knees taking little fluttery steps.

'Who is she?' I shouted over the record.

'No idea. Someone brought her back after the pub. Maybe she came with Nick.'

She seemed in a world of her own and oblivious to any of us, so I went over to where Nick was standing. Andy had met Nick at a demo the year before. He stood out amongst the people I knew as being 'posh'. Obviously public school educated (I got it out of him that he went to Dulwich College), he seemed like a fish out of water. He once mentioned that he didn't get on with his parents and I wondered if he had been chucked out.

'Did you bring her, Nick?' I said, jerking my head at pixie girl.

'Yes—is that a problem?' he said with a slight stammer, looking anxious.

'No, of course not. I just wondered who she was.'

We were all very casual about who came in and out of our places. It was part of the squatting ethos. I wondered if Nick fancied his luck with her and persisted in asking him questions.

He fascinated me and Tessa as he was so different from the other blokes, and I wanted to report any gossip back to her.

'How do you know her then?'

Nick was in agony at my interrogation, but I ignored that. I needed answers.

'Erm, she lives near my family,' he managed to squeeze out.

That's when I realised we had another posho on our hands.

'What's her name?'

'Not sure.'

'Is she staying with you tonight?'

That was too much for Nick and he spluttered a bit and waved his hands about but couldn't actually come up with a coherent answer. When the music stopped she came over and sat next to him and they started an earnest conversation lying on the floor.

I suddenly slumped. I had been working all evening and had a shift the next day. The problem with the dancing Tuesdays was that they took place in our room. I decided to take the same attitude as in the pub, 'OK you lot, that's enough. I need to go to bed. Everyone out.'

Joe raised his eyebrows at me but seemed happy to call it a night as well. With a few grumbles and moans the group shuffled out and I picked up some glasses and emptied overflowing ashtrays. Joe unpegged the lampshade and we went to bed.

* * *

The house was light and airy. It didn't have the damp smell that Farquhar Road had. It was made for summer living with wooden floorboards everywhere and a window halfway up the stairs that

47

opened onto the flat roof. In the basement, Ryan had a mini zoo that spilled out on the back garden. It was out of bounds to us as one of his Alsatians was moody.

'Christ, Ryan, it nearly savaged me when I went out to the bin,' Joe shouted.

'Well, he would do that. He thinks you're an intruder.'

'Can't you tell them we're OK or something? I'd like to keep my legs.'

Ryan often escaped from his zoo and spent time in our kitchen, which was just above the back garden. Sometimes he would open the window and suspend a can of dog food with one end opened over the prowling Alsatians below.

'Here you are, darlings,' he would say and the gloopy mass slithered out and a horrible snarling and slurping sound ensued below. Most of the time they were his babies but other times he was glummer about his menagerie.

'They've just done a packet in the living room,' he would say and sit brooding the clean up job he had to do, blowing the steam off his tea, precariously balanced on a stool by the yellow Formica table.

It was inevitable that we would come to the attention of the neighbours. We always did. The pounding up and down the wooden staircases, music, dancing Tuesdays, and the animals made confrontation inevitable. The first thing the neighbours did was put broken glass up on their dividing wall in the garden. We ignored that. It was a lovely hot summer and Joe spent time lugging earth and wood up to the flat roof and made a garden of sorts with three little flowerbeds. We planted sunflowers and they soon provided a screen of sorts that hid the dope smoking from the neighbours. We spent hours out there on hot summer days and evenings drinking, smoking, and listening to my cassettes. It was amazing how many people we could fit in the small area.

Because the dogs roamed free in the garden, and the neighbours had taken to patrolling and shouting insults over the walls, we abandoned the garden and crowded on to the makeshift patio out of the way of the local hostility.

Ryan had added an abandoned puppy to his zoo but the bigger dogs didn't like her. I brought her upstairs for a cuddle and pleaded with Joe for us to take the little thing on.

'Are you sure we can look after her? We'll have to take her for walks. She can't use the garden and she'll have to get on with the cat.'

'I can take her out when I come in from work and first thing before I go,' I said. 'She's so gorgeous and those Alsatians will savage her. I grew up with a dog like her, look at her little face.'

Joe rubbed her silky ears. I could see that he was smitten and pressed home my advantage. 'What will happen to her if we don't take her on?'

We did take her on and called her Lucy. She was a sweet-natured little Labrador puppy who happily pottered up and down the wooden stairs following us around and only had the rare accident. 'Has she done a packet?' Ryan would ask when he saw her.

Around this time the neighbours devised a new strategy. They called the RSPCA to come out and inspect Ryan's animals. To their chagrin the whole pack were given a clean bill of health.

'Anything else around?' the guy asked. I think he quite enjoyed visiting our house of alternative strangeness. 'You might as well get them all out for me as they'll only call me again.'

I picked up Lucy who had been lying asleep making little snory noises and whimpering as though catching rabbits in her dreams. 'Just our cat, Big Puss. I don't know if you'll be able to see her as she's hiding. There's also our little puppy, Lucy.'

'I won't worry about the cat, but hello Lucy,' he said. 'Let's have a look at you. How has she been, has she had her jabs?'

I looked down, embarrassed. 'I was going to take her when I got paid so not yet. She's OK, but a little quiet recently and slightly off her food.'

He spent quite a long time checking her, more than he had spent on Ryan's dogs. One of them he had just looked at through the window, as she was quite savage with strangers. When he finished, his jovial air had gone and he stared at us like a head teacher. 'I don't like the look of her,' he said. 'You need to take her to the vet.'

'We haven't got enough money for that,' Joe said.

I felt bad and stroked Lucy's head looking at the man imploringly. Joe's voice was shaking, and I knew he felt upset as well.

'Take her to the free vet if you're on the dole.'

He definitely wasn't as friendly now. Joe was signing on, but I wasn't. When the door slammed behind him, we looked at each other aghast.

'We have to find out where it is and take her now. I'll call in sick from work.'

We found the address from the telephone book and took the bus to the vet. We sat side by side on the downstairs long seat holding hands with Lucy on our lap. I felt churned up inside and guilty.

Chapter Six

When we got home I felt so overwhelmed with grief that I knocked on Tessa's door, burst into tears, and lay on her bed.

'Poor Lucy, and poor you,' she said, sitting cross-legged, reading and smoking. Joe hovered in the doorway. Tessa waved him away.

'Was it awful?' she said. I tried to speak but just kept gulping and crying. I put my head in her lap and got tears all over her cheesecloth skirt. 'Ssssh,' she said, stroking my forehead and flicking fag ash on my hair. 'It'll all be OK.'

I sniffed and slumped against her, picking at her candlewick bedspread. Tessa felt like home. She wasn't someone I had just met, in contrast to everyone else in my new life. Even Joe, although he was my boyfriend, I hadn't known him for long. I had seen Tess's smile since I was eight, and at the moment she was the stability and familiarity that I craved.

'The vet had a good look at her, but it was too late,' I managed to get out. Tessa put her arm around me.

'It's our job as pet owners,' she said and looked into my eyes. 'You know that; they can't tell us themselves. We have to do it for them.'

This was something Tessa passionately believed in and repeated often. When she moved into the house she gave Ryan a long grilling over how he treated his animals. I thought bitterly that it should have been me that she questioned.

'And now little Lucy is running free in a lovely field somewhere and has no pain. She's probably with Honey right now,' Tessa said.

That was too much for me. Honey was my childhood dog that died a few years ago. She had been put down as well. The thought of Honey and Lucy together, both blond Labradors, made me sob convulsively. Snot ran out of my nose and down my face. Tessa handed me a grubby tissue. I blew hard and sat up properly. I felt completely drained.

'The thing is, Tessa, we were going to give her the jabs but we didn't have the bread and we were waiting until Joe got his dole.'

As I spoke a small part of me wondered if that was true. With so many other things to spend our modest capital on — dope, drink, music, food even — would we really have given up some of it to get jabs for a puppy that didn't seem ill?

'Of course you were,' Tessa said, and I was comforted. If Tessa believed that we would have done the right thing then I believed her.

Joe came back in and sat beside me. He looked drained and I thought he had probably gone off somewhere for a cry as well. Joe wasn't one of those men who didn't cry, he had an active sensitive side and showed it often. I knew this had hit him hard. We hadn't said anything on the bus home, as I couldn't trust myself not to start keening loudly in public. I just kept seeing her little body on the operating table and the quiver that had run through her as the vet put the needle into her tiny beige body. She had come into the vets with us so trusting, her little tail wagging when he stroked her. I had cradled her tiny head and told her 'I'm sorry Looby Loo' as her short life stopped.

'What were we thinking?' Joe said. 'We can barely take care of ourselves let alone a puppy.'

He was right but I couldn't hear it at that moment. I shook his hand off and said, 'I'm going to make a cup of tea. And some toast.'

Tessa looked at Joe, still slumped on the bed. 'Come on you two,' she said. 'You should be together in this.'

I turned round to Joe and held out my hand. 'Coming?'

That evening the house gang sat around in our room, the nearest thing to a living room we had. Word had got round about poor Lucy and they all drifted in. Andy brought a bottle of fruit wine. It was disgusting but the cheapest, strongest alcohol around so we had all got used to the slightly cough syrup taste. Ryan brought one of his dogs to cheer me up but had to take it away after it started sniffing frantically around the room and driving us all mad. Nick passed around a packet of biscuits and Tessa contributed some fruit and nut chocolate.

The house gossip was about the three drug dealers who had moved in opposite us in the past few days. 'More tough guys from Glasgow. That's just what we need,' Joe said, surely thinking of Gene.

'Oh, they're not too bad,' Andy said.

'That's only because you went to score and they gave you a freebie,' Tessa said.

'Who do you get it from? Is there a dealer or is it all of them?' Nick said.

'Just knock on the door and ask for Ginger. He's the least scary and the only one who sells dope,' Andy said.

'What do the others sell then?' Nick said.

'Oh, I don't know, shed loads of speed and heroin probably.'

Someone knocked on the front door in a rapping pattern that meant it was a friend. It was Jacob, a new addition to our circle who had recently moved into a local squat with his wife and baby. Joe knew him from a previous squat. Tessa must have told him about Lucy because he came straight over, sat down next to me on the floor and swept me into an embrace. I smelt patchouli and cigarette smoke as his slight body pressed against me.

Tessa tried not to smirk and Joe looking slightly pissed off. Married or not, Tessa and I both had a crush on Jacob. He was charismatic and always seemed focused on women, talking to any female in the room with great interest, drawing them in like a magnet. We rarely saw his wife, Tina, or his child.

Later that night as we were getting ready for bed, after chucking everyone out at a late hour, Joe said, 'He's still a wrong'un.'

'Why?' I said, desperate for gossip to relay to Tessa.

'Tell you in the morning,' he said getting under the blankets and soon I could hear him breathing heavily. I felt annoyed that he was able to go to sleep so quickly, but the dope going around that evening had smelt strong so I knew why.

Awake and anxious, the house creaked and I listened to the traffic outside, lights coming in through our bare windows. I lay there fretting about Lucy and trying to get into a comfortable position. Joe seemed all arms and legs and I couldn't fit round him like I usually did. I resented his ability to switch off.

Big Puss sensed my sadness and jumped onto the bed purring like a little steam engine. She turned around and around and finally settled in between us, adding to my physical discomfort but soothing my soul. I stroked her head. 'Joe are you awake?' I said and pressed a finger into his back. I knew he wasn't, but I felt alone in my insomnia and wanted company.

His weight shifted as he surfaced from sleep and turned towards me.

'Mind Big Puss,' I said.

'What is it for fucks sake? I'm knackered.'

'Billy's dog had all those puppies.'

'No,' he said and turned back again, sighing.

He was probably right. I just wanted to do it all again but the correct way this time.

The next day Jacob came around. He didn't ever come to the house on his own, and he rarely came with his family, but he had a sidekick, a bloke called Matt. He was Scottish with a soft Highland burr, thin and nervy looking, but I quickly discovered he had a kind heart. A heart that Joe said was being taken advantage of by Jacob.

'I'm so sorry to hear about Lucy,' Matt said. He hugged me too, but I didn't enjoy it as much as Jacob's. His clothes smelled like they hadn't been dried properly underlain with sharp notes of body odor.

'Thanks, Matt, do you want a cup of tea?'

'Oh, never mind about that, darling,' Jacob said. 'He hasn't got time. Matt, you're going over the road to score from Ginger. Have you got enough bread?'

'Sure,' Matt said, patting his trousers and disappearing.

'What you need to cheer you up is a party,' Jacob said. 'You haven't had a moving in party yet, why don't you have one this Saturday?'

I shrugged. I wasn't working that weekend but I didn't want to sound too eager as I still felt sad about Lucy.

'Cool idea, man,' Joe said.

'I don't want those guys over the road coming,' I said.

'It's going to be hard to stop them. They'll see what's going on,' Joe said.

After a while Matt reappeared.

'If you want anything moved or sorted out Matt will help, won't you?' Jacob said.

'Sure,' Matt said.

Jacob pushed his hand through his thick curly dark hair.

'OK we have to split now. My old lady is in from work and needs to crash, and I've got to look after the little one,' Jacob said. He had a rueful look as he went down the stairs that I thought was charming.

'More likely it'll be Matt looking after the baby,' Joe said as the front door closed. 'Jacob's always been like that — good fun but selfish. He has a knack of getting other people to do what he should be doing, especially chicks.'

'I think it's lovely how Jacob supports Tina with the baby,' I said, defiantly.

Joe raised his eyebrows but said nothing.

'Joe's so down on Jacob,' I said to Tessa later that day. The first time I met Jacob he sat and talked to me and Tessa at great length, asking us questions and showing a real interest in our lives. 'Here he goes again,' I heard Joe mutter.

Of course after that first meeting Tessa and I wondered about Tina. She was a petite Greek woman with a pixie cut, always sounded slightly breathless and talked nineteen to the dozen. The first time we met her, she was restless and constantly moving around the kitchen as she spoke to us. We had gone there to see the baby but really hoping to see Jacob.

He wasn't in. Tina seemed relieved to see us and confessed that looking after her child bored her. 'I'm just so tired after work,' she wailed.

Tessa and I nodded sympathetically.

'Do you like her name?' she said, peering into our eyes.

I had the distinct feeling that if we said no she would change it.

'I wanted to call her Gýftos. It means gypsy in Greek but Jacob wouldn't have it. He said he'd leave me,' she said.

I was sure she was exaggerating.

With baby in her arms, Tessa looked over at me and raised her eyebrows.

As Tina pottered around the kitchen picking up and putting down cups, reminding me of a woodland sprite, I decided I couldn't bear the employment mystery any longer. 'So what work exactly do you do?'

With a broom in her hands, looking as if surprised to see it, she brushed the floor in a desultory way and said, 'Oh, you know.'

Having got this far I was determined to get to the truth. Spurred on by the presence of Tessa, who was feeding the tot from a bottle, and realising that Tina knew she was hemmed in, I stared at her. She propped the broom against the wall, raised her hands above her head and executed a neat twirl. 'I dance,' she said. Then she looked at us and said, 'and now I sleep.' Without asking, she pushed past me and Tessa to the stairs. We listened and heard her tripping up the uncarpeted steps.

'Well,' Tessa said, and sat down on a wooden chair, the baby still latched onto the bottle. 'She didn't even ask if it was OK?'

'Arty types, eh?' I said.

'A dancer,' Tessa said. 'Do you think she meant ballet?'

I thought back to the twirl. It had seemed quite professional.

'Possibly.'

'I thought you had to be taller?'

I wandered around Tina's house, nosing and hoping Tessa didn't ask me to hold the baby. Despite looking after my younger brother quite a bit, I wasn't sure with babies. Once I had been left in charge of the child of a friend and it had rolled off the sofa onto the floor. Screaming as I desperately tried to hush it, I was frightened that I'd be blamed for my inattention. That had shaken my confidence. In contrast, Tessa held the little one like a true professional.

'Did you know Jacob wants us to all move in round here?' I said. 'I mean I really love Camden Hill Road but if we did have to move it would be nice here.'

'I bet we'd be landed with this one a lot,' Tessa said, jiggling the baby.

'My stepfather Monty only knows two things to do to entertain babies,' I said.

'Well try them,' Tessa said, starting to lose her patience.

I filled my cheeks with air and blew out making a trumpeting sound.

The child looked astonished, her rosebud mouth formed a little round, and she stared at us and stopped crying. Gradually she fell asleep.

'Phew,' Tessa said, looking for somewhere to put her. 'What's the other thing he does?'

'He gives them his keys.'

We sat in silence, too scared to move much or talk in case she woke up again. I went into the living room but there was very little in there and nowhere safe to put a baby. It all seemed a bit ramshackle, and even though it was pretty, there was a distinct lack of practicality. I walked back into the kitchen and said to Tessa, 'Apparently all this buying special things for a baby is a load of nonsense.'

'All you need is a dry drawer lined with a blanket and a baby is perfectly happy,' Tessa said.

We both looked around the kitchen for anything that fitted that description but couldn't even see a kettle. Tina hadn't offered us a cup of tea when we had arrived, just thrust the baby at Tessa.

Footsteps echoed in the hallway and Jacob appeared. Wearing a pale blue Shetland wool jumper, a little small for him, with his elbows poking through holes and jeans ripped at the knees, I longed to patch everything up for him. Expecting him to relieve us of duty, we stood up. Tessa was clutching the sweaty and sleeping child who I realised was producing something smelly.

'Oh lovely, lovely girls,' he said. 'Could you just hang on for a bit? I've got something I need to do. Thanks, you're amazing.'

With that he winked at us and rushed upstairs. After a pause we heard his voice and Tina's and the unmistakable sound of her laughter and a couple settling in to have sex.

Tessa and I looked at each other in bewilderment as the baby started to squirm. We heard more footsteps in the hall and Matt appeared. 'Where's Jacob?' he said.

I jerked my head up to the ceiling. Matt heard the noises and blushed. 'Oh, OK, I get it,' he said.

Before he could say anything more, Tessa shoved the wriggling and smelly baby at him. 'Cheers, Matt. We've got to rush and she needs her nappy changing. Come on, Deb.'

Tessa grabbed my hand and pulled me out, leaving Matt standing in the kitchen holding the struggling tot and looking bewildered.

Chapter Seven

1977 was a great summer. There wasn't the high temperatures of 1976 but it was hot. The charts were full of rubbish except for two songs that we played on repeat: 'Exodus' by Bob Marley and the Wailers and 'God Save the Queen' by the Sex Pistols.

Music was changing, the pomp and nonsense of the supergroups giving way to the idea that anyone could form a band. Andy continued to be my music guru and was constantly saying 'listen to this' and introducing me to new bands. The hippy clothes and culture that I was comfortable with was replaced with punk. Although I felt a little old for it at 20, I was willing to change and embrace the newness.

At the house things were changing too. It took a while before the penny dropped about Matt but eventually it did. I had grown up with older gay men. My mother loved the showbiz life. She was friends with Danny La Rue and gay men loved her. She also had some lesbian friends and used to go to the famous club Gateways and cause a stir with her pretty blond looks and trendy clothes.

The gay men that my mother knew were single and constantly in love with some unsuitable married straight man who was in the closet and just wanted sex. They would come round and cry on my mother's shoulder and she would dispense sympathy and gin.

The idea of a gay man who was my contemporary took a while to sink in, but slowly I realised that Matt was in love with Jacob and that Jacob was well aware of this and used it to his advantage.

'Bit bloody obvious,' Joe said when I mentioned this to him.

Jacob was unquestionably heterosexual, but occasionally would throw Matt a bone and put an arm round his shoulders or drunkenly tell him what a good mate he was. But that was all.

'Oh, I think there's more,' Joe said and tapped the side of his nose. 'I think he gives him the odd hand job.' I was shocked and didn't want to think that my crush had feet of clay.

A couple of weeks later, we had the party that Jacob had suggested. It was a hit. There were crowds in our room, the kitchen, and out on the little roof garden as well. Friends, friends of friends, and complete strangers poured into the house. The windows were open and the neighbours were furious but we didn't care.

We knew that our days at the house were numbered. It was privately owned and the landlord had come round trying to intimidate us into leaving. Joe had done his usual shtick but it wasn't working. The owner went straight to the courts. The summons arrived and we knew it was a matter of weeks before we were packing our bags, so we were going to make the best of it.

'Where shall we go?' I said to Joe.

'Jacob really wants us to move down near him. There's some good houses around there. He's found one next door to some cool black dude called Winston in Sainsbury Road and the people living there now are moving out in a few weeks. If we get in quick, then it won't be damp or have smashed windows or anything.'

'What about if we have to go before then?'

'Over the road will have us.'

'I suppose.'

'Over the road' meant the run-down terrace house squat with an outside toilet next to the drug dealers. I wasn't that keen on the couple who lived there. They were older than us. The woman had a sweet face marred by missing teeth and a resigned and defeated air. He had rakish good looks but a permanent scowl. I thought they were connected to the dealers next door as they both seemed heavily into drugs and generally quite out of it. However, their squat was a port in a storm and I hoped we wouldn't have to be there long.

They were both at the party which was turning into a sort of farewell do, a goodbye to the house. Nick had gone and Andy was moving out of the area. He was at art college and only moved this far away because of Joe. I would miss him, my passport to punk and new wave music. We were a team at the party trying to get 'our' music played.

'Fucking Free?' Tom said in disgust. 'If that were mine, I'd melt it and use it as an ashtray.'

The owner of the record tried to put up a fight.

'You can dance to it man,' he muttered as he shuffled away.

Andy would allow Motown, so we mainly played that, my favourite.

'The old stuff though, Northern soul,' warned Andy. 'Not disco shite.'

Moving between our room and the roof garden, I was waylaid by Matt on the turn of the stairs. He was quite out of it, swaying with a joint in his hand. And he had a silly grin on his face, which was uncommon as I rarely saw him smile.

'You looking for Jacob?' I said, only because I had seen him holding court in the garden.

'Fuck Jacob,' Matt slurred. 'I'm fed up with him. Fed up being his little tame bum boy.'

I was shocked. Matt never referred to his sexuality and never had a bad word to say about Jacob.

'Are you OK, Matt?' I said.

He propped himself up against the wall and smiled at me.

'Better than OK,' he said, offering the joint to me. I waved it away and watched as he crushed it out on the floor.

'I've always liked you,' he said.

'Oh, that's lovely. I've always liked you as well.'

He took a step towards me and said, 'No, I mean, I've always really liked you. You're kind to me.'

I started to feel a sense of alarm and tried to step back, but Matt had wedged me into a corner. He loomed over me and said, 'So lovely.' To my horror I realised that he was going to try and kiss me. His lips made an ineffectual attempt to cover mine. I squirmed and moved my head aside. I didn't want to be horrible to him but also wasn't enjoying this one little bit. I wished Joe would appear, but for a crowded party we seemed to have found an isolated spot.

'Mmmm,' Matt said as he continued to lunge at me. I felt his tongue and was horrified. I put a hand on his chest to push him back and he swayed with his head hanging.

'Matt, this isn't what you want, is it?'

He covered his face with his hands and started to sob.

'I'm fed up with it,' he said through his fingers.

I felt completely out of my depth and had no idea what to do. Looking round frantically for Joe, I felt a hand on my shoulder and turned to find Jacob. He quickly sized up the situation and put his arm round Matt, drawing his head to his chest and making comforting crooning noises.

'Didn't mean it,' Matt whispered.

'I know you didn't, man. Now stop crying, you're OK. We'll go and light one up, eh?'

I wriggled away and with relief made my way onto the roof terrace pulling in lungs of fresh night air.

Joe was sitting on the edge of the flower bed balanced precariously. When he saw me, he stood up and beamed drunkenly, 'Look what I can do.' Then he turned, unzipped his trousers and pissed a huge arc into the sky. The crowd standing around all cheered. Annoyed, I left and went back to our room to listen to music. There was no sign of Jacob or Matt.

I found Nick sitting on our mattress looking a bit fed up.

'I went over the road to score but no one was there,' he said.

I told him I had just seen one of the dealers on the roof terrace and his face brightened. Then he loped off. I knew that Nick battled with his need to buy dope and his fear of the tough dealers over the road. He had obviously come from a privileged background and tried to hide it. There was no mistaking his public-school accent though. He got the piss taken out of him constantly, especially by Joe who was an Essex boy.

Nick was a soft-spoken sensitive soul who was desperate to be with 'the people' as he called us. I summed him up as a posh socialist who wanted to connect with a working-class lifestyle in an act of rebellion. Tessa and I were always trying to match-make him with single girls but to no avail. Tessa wasn't interested in him. Her taste ran more to bad boys like Jacob.

Out the bedroom window I saw Nick go over the road with the ginger dealer. 'Finally, he's getting to score,' I thought. The party carried on until the early hours, and it was only a neighbour banging on our door and threatening to call the police that brought it to a close. I was mooching around picking up old bottles and emptying ashtrays, and Joe was still outside on the roof chatting when I heard the front door and Nick came back in. He passed me on the stairs and looked even more drawn than usual.

'Alright, Nick?' I said, but he didn't seem to hear me and carried on upstairs to his room. That would be the last time I would see him.

Joe was fast asleep when I left for work. It had been a struggle to get up after only three hours sleep. As a result I was a bit late and rushed out of the house barely dressed. After I finished my shift, I came home and found Joe in the kitchen making tea and toast. The house felt quiet.

'Where is everyone?' I said.

'Tessa is in her room,' Joe said.

'And Nick and Andy?'

Joe paused and fished a tea bag out of my mug. I sat down at the kitchen table, landing with a thump. I had been on my feet all day and we had been busy. With only a few hours sleep I was knackered and looking forward to a bath. I knew there was no bathroom in the house we were going to and was determined to make the most of this one however many kettles of hot water I had to fill.

Joe hadn't answered my question, so I looked at him enquiringly.

'Nick and Andy?' I repeated.

'Something bad happened last night, babe,' he said.

I felt sick, a horrible feeling in the pit of my stomach.

'Is it Big Puss?' I said, my voice quavering.

'No, it's much worse than that.'

65

'Just fucking tell me.'

'It's Nick.'

'Has he died?'

'No, he hasn't but he's left. Andy took him back to his folks. He's in a pretty bad way.'

'What happened?'

'He went over to score with the ginger bloke and the other dealers were there. They were bad men, Deb. I said they were bad men all along,' Joe said and stopped. He sounded on the verge of tears.

'Anyway, you know what Nick's like. It was hard to get any sense out of him this morning. Apparently, they all started to take the piss out of him because of the way he spoke. Then they got chummy with him, like he was a little pet. Andy found him crying in his bedroom this morning.'

I felt a sense of dread. Joe carried on, wanting to get the story over and done with.

'They mixed up some speed with water and made him drink it and then they raped him. He told Andy. I made him a cup of tea and he just sat in the kitchen. It was horrible. Andy got him together and took him back to his parents.'

I was silent. I couldn't find the words to express how I felt.

'All of them raped him?' I croaked.

'Ginger says no, not him. He said he was upstairs, that he wasn't involved.'

'Do you believe him?'

'He came over an hour ago to see how Nick was. The other two have gone back up the road today and he's splitting soon as well. They got a court order to leave the other day, same landlord as us so we'll be next. He tried to give Nick some hash as a leaving present.'

I spluttered over my tea.

'Oh, that's good of him. The whole thing is his fucking fault. I saw Nick coming in but had no idea. He just rushed up to his room. I just thought he wanted to have a quiet spliff.'

'Ginger seemed genuinely upset by the whole thing.'

'I don't care. He's never coming in any house that I'm in again, or any of the others if they come back. I don't want you scoring off them either.'

'Well, they're all leaving anyway.'

'Good riddance.'

Tears dripped down my cheeks. I was in shock. It made me think again of Jill and what she had been through.

'Do you think his parents will want to involve the pigs?' I said.

'I doubt it. Even if he tells them they'll want to hush it up, I would think. Probably send him to some expensive clinic somewhere to get over it.'

I sniffed and rubbed my face on the back of my arm. Joe leant over and patted me.

'I liked Nick. He was so sweet,' I said.

'I know, he never really fitted in though.'

Joe bumped into Nick a few years later. They were on a bus together and Nick seemed really out of it.

'He didn't recognise me,' Joe said. 'I was really upset because we had been quite close in 34. He just sat there rummaging through his bag and eventually he got out a matchbox and showed it to me as his prize possession.'

'What was in there?'

'A dead stag beetle.'

We sat in silence for a while. Joe squeezed my hand.

'Poor bugger,' he said.

There was little time to think about what happened to Nick. A few days after the party we got a court summons. When we appeared before the magistrate, he gave us some harsh words and no notice so we came home and instantly started packing.

I loved this bright clean house with a bathroom and a roof garden. Everyone there made it such a special place. And it had been a great summer. But I had sad memories as well. Poor Lucy and the horrible news about Nick. Yet again I wanted to move on and start over. I was fed up with these abrupt and nasty endings and wanted to make sure the house in Sainsbury Road would be a happy home even with no bathroom and an outside bog.

I decided this was a good time to shed my hippy exterior and make a new start. I sold or gave away my wrap around skirts and cheesecloth shirts. I cut my hair. I was even more certain that old music was dead, so I sold or gave away even more of my vinyl. We had less to pack that way.

I was dreading moving over the road while we waited for Sainsbury Road to empty. It was kind of them to offer but I felt like I was leaving a sunny haven to go to a dank underworld.

'Oh, for fuck's sake,' Joe said. I could tell he was exasperated. 'Don't be all doom and gloom. It's going to be fine.'

But it wasn't.

Chapter Eight

It didn't take long to move. We just had to carry everything over the road, but it felt a huge distance in other ways. We were now living with strangers. I missed the light, space, and bathroom in our old squat.

The new house was cold and drab. Summer was over and our room smelt damp. Going outside to the toilet wasn't easy, and there were no hot baths.

'They've not even been there,' Joe said. He was obsessed with the fact that we had moved in a hurry with the court order and then nothing had happened to the house. 'They're just going to chuck that roof garden down. I sweated buckets getting earth up there and now it's going to be ruined.'

One day we heard a racket and went outside to see what was going on. It wasn't the owners but lads who were taking everything they could from 34 to sell for scrap. It sounded like they were smashing up the place. Saddened, we went back inside.

'Bastards,' muttered Joe. 'They just want to get whatever they can. There was no need to do that and give us a bad name.'

We believed that living in empty houses was a political act, that houses shouldn't be empty. We put up with the lack of amenities for rent free accommodation and tried to make sure we lived in them respectfully and left everything in good nick.

Andy moved to Wimbledon to be closer to the art college. He had put up with the long journey because of the house but now that that was gone there was no need to stick around. He started doing gigs on the alternative comedy circuit and told us sometime later that he had seen the ginger drug dealer there and that he had an Equity card!

Sitting in a pub in Brixton, waiting for Andy to go on, I screamed in disbelief at this news. I had stayed true to my word and Ginger was not allowed anywhere near me after poor Nick.

'I know, jammy bastard,' Andy said. 'He did bit parts, you know, playing hard men in soaps and stuff like that.'

'Huh, true to type then,' I snorted.

'Truth is stranger than fiction,' he said, downed his beer and went backstage.

It was harder to get on in the new house with just the two of us. Joe and I were used to being with friends. Being thrown together with this new group of strangers grated on both of us. I really missed the Tuesday night dances. The Misery Couple (as I had christened them) and the other people in the house didn't have a lot of lightness to them. Life seemed harder in the new place. I hadn't grown up with a role model of a functional relationship and I don't think Joe had either.

The first time I went to Joe's rambling Victorian family home in Romford we were on a train and a typical city gent sitting opposite us lowered his newspaper and said, 'Aren't you my son?' It was his dad. His mum was friendly but distracted and he had lots of sisters and a twin brother with special needs who he didn't talk about much.

My family liked Joe and he was included in our gatherings, but I didn't see them often. They had their world of market trading, boozing, and friends, and I had mine.

Mr and Mrs Misery were friendly, but I didn't like them.

'Got any fags?' Mr Misery said as soon as we moved in.

'Can I borrow some of your tea bags?' Mrs Misery said as I arranged our provisions on the kitchen shelves. I knew they were being kind by letting us stay but I couldn't warm to them and also distrusted them.

'Not long now,' Jacob kept saying but nothing materialized, and I thought we might be there until Christmas. I still saw Tessa. She had moved in with her new boyfriend. I met him the same time as she did, a couple of months earlier.

Tessa and I had heard there was a squat down Gatestone Road and wanted to visit. They were huge Edwardian villas, bigger than anything we had lived in. We were a bit drunk that night, walking down the road shouting, 'Come on where are you? Come out, screamers!'

'It's more of a commune,' Tessa said. 'They do something called Primal Scream.'

'What's that when it's at home?' I said.

'You scream and scream and get all of your feelings out and then you feel better.'

'Huh, my mum did that all the time with my stepdad.'

'Yes, but that was when she was pissed.'

The screamers had a rule that you couldn't visit them between certain hours in the evening, but we had forgotten the time. They also had a secret bell, but we didn't know where that was either.

'Come on, I think it's this one,' I said and strode up the pathway of a house that looked more disheveled and squattish than the others.

'What about the bell?' Tessa said.

'Oh, sod that. Everyone always likes to see chicks,' I said, and knocked using the huge carved knocker. I also rang the bell on the door for good measure. Then, frightened momentarily at my confidence, I stood back and huddled at the corner of the step with Tessa.

Nothing happened for a while.

'I heard they've got a padded cell,' I whispered to Tessa, and we both stifled nervous giggles. We heard footsteps inside and clutched each other.

The footsteps stopped and a voice said, 'Who is that?'

'That's Franz,' whispered Tessa.

'It's us, Deb and Tessa, from the pub the other night. You said to pop round and see the squat,' I shouted.

'Oh cool,' the voice replied and the door swung open.

Franz was an archetypal hippy, at least ten years older than us, with a full beard and long hair. He wore a faded blue T-shirt and old jeans.

'What did I say about chicks?' I muttered to Tessa. She poked me with her elbow and we giggled as we followed Franz inside.

Off the hall and behind big wooden doors, a huge room ran the whole length of the house divided by folding doors. It had high ceilings with elaborate moulding and ceiling roses. I could imagine it full of heavy Edwardian furniture, a butler throwing open the folding doors to reveal a dining table set for dinner. In contrast, one of the rooms was empty and the other had two mattresses pushed up against a wall with cheap Indian throws over them. Instead of swags and flounces, another Indian throw was nailed up at the window. The best thing about it was a little stove that had been installed in front of the once imposing white marble fireplace. The whole place smelt of incense and dope.

Next to the rooms was a tiny kitchen with an electric cooker going full blast, heating it to a cosy fug. It had a table, a fifties storage unit with a pull-down front, a Baby Belling two-ring electric cooker, and a couple of chairs jammed against the wall.

'Living room, kitchen,' Franz said. He pointed upstairs. 'My room and Mik's room.'

I looked at Tessa.

'Mind if we have an explore?'

Franz shrugged.

'Be my guest.'

Climbing the creaky wooden staircase, we bypassed Mik and Franz's rooms and carried on to the top of the house. The main rooms were abandoned, one had a broken window and a huge pile of broken furniture. A ragged curtain fluttered in the wind, and it smelled of damp. I shivered.

Tessa opened another door. It was a smaller room with the floor, walls, window, and ceiling covered in dusty brown felt and egg cartons.

'This is the padded cell for the screaming! I heard about this, bloody creepy or what?'

She carried out an experimental shout. The sound was dull and flat. We went back downstairs and found Franz in the kitchen rolling a joint and making tea. I sat down, but Tessa carried on wandering around.

'Where does that door go to?' she said.

'Down to the basement,' Franz said. 'Johnny lives there. Go down if you want. I think he's in.'

The door opened and I heard Tessa going down the stairs then a muffled man's voice and Tessa's higher tones. She didn't return for ages. I was getting fed up with waving away Franz's joint and our stilted conversation. I was suspicious of his beatific

Jesus hippy aura and the awkward way he was chatting me up. I kept mentioning Joe and then, bored, I got up and started prowling around the two big rooms.

'It would be a great place for a party,' I shouted. 'Loads of room to dance.' He didn't respond, and I wondered if parties were against the screamers' ethos or something.

Just as I was about to desert Tessa and go home, she emerged from the basement. Slightly flushed, and chatting to the tall guy that followed her, she introduced me. I liked him better than Franz; he didn't have a beard and spoke with soft northern tones. He nodded at Tessa as we headed out the door.

'See you Monday then,' he said.

I waited until we were properly out of earshot then grabbed Tessa.

'Tell all.'

'Well, he's lovely. You should see his place downstairs, it's great. He has his own kitchen and a weird kind of bathroom that's rigged up with a tank and stuff. He's very clever with things like that. There's all sorts downstairs.'

'Does he work?'

'No, he's on the dole, but he's got this great plan for making and selling bird houses. I'm sure he'll do well.'

She sounded enthusiastic. I caught a whiff of something from her on the night air.

'Have you been drinking?'

She looked down at her feet.

'Yes, he gave me some home brew. He makes all of his own.'

I was furious.

'You could've got me down there. I was stuck upstairs with Jesus and his dope talking endlessly about Red Leb.'

'I know why he's called Franz.'

I stopped, instantly agog.

'He's from the Channel Islands and had a German nanny. She called him that because he reminded her of her little brother who had died in the war, and it stuck. I think his real name is Fred.'

'Has he got a girlfriend?'

'Who? Franz? Why, are you interested?'

I kicked her sideways and she laughed, knowing full well who I meant.

'Well, I'm not sure. He mentioned a woman called Julie, but she's got no chance against my feminine wiles. We're meeting at the cheap night on Monday at your pub. Usually he only goes to real ale pubs, but he said he'd make an exception for me.'

She gave me a look.

'See, I told you. Feminine wiles.'

And so it proved true. Shortly after that Johnny and Tessa became an item. Then she moved in with him downstairs in the screamers' basement.

'What about the screaming time?' I asked.

'Oh, they do it now and then but it's not that important apparently.'

* * *

We settled into our slightly damp room and tried to get along with the Miseries. As we waited to hear about Sainsbury Road, one weekend there was an ad hoc party after the pub. I was struggling with dreadful period pains and not pleased when I came home to a load of strangers and loud music. Wandering into the living room, Mrs Misery grabbed me by the arm.

75

Feverish and overly excited, she pulled me over to where a thin young girl was sitting.

'Deb, say hi to Jody. She's run away from home just round the corner from where I'm from.'

I tried to muster up some enthusiasm. Jody had a sweet smile, and I could see it was important to Mrs Misery who I knew felt homesick for Newcastle.

'Have you seen Joe?' I said, but they were both chatting nine to the dozen about where they lived so I left them to it.

I walked up the stairs rubbing my stomach and wondering if I could just make a hot water bottle and go to bed. In our room I found Joe and an unknown bloke playing guitar.

'That's all I need,' I thought.

They were trying to work out the chords to 'Hotel California' and playing the same bit over and over again. I lay on the bed and groaned but they both ignored me. I tried again.

'You OK, babe?' Joe said. The bloke ignored me.

'I'm in agony and I just want to go to bed. But I want a hot water bottle and a cup of tea — any chance? I can't face going back down there.'

Joe put down his guitar, came over and patted my head.

'Sure thing, I've run out of fags anyway. I'll nip down and be back in a minute.'

He disappeared and I looked over at the unknown player who seemed to be in a finger picking reverie. I couldn't be bothered to hassle him, and it was quite melodic and soothing. I took some clothes off under the blanket and then got into bed, hoping Joe wouldn't take long. There was just a side light on, and I was adept at going to sleep in lighted rooms, so I soon dozed off.

I woke up with a start. Joe came in and I had a sense that time had passed. The unknown bloke was crouched by the lamp reading one of our books. Joe knelt on the bed and passed me a lukewarm hot water bottle but no tea.

'How are you feeling?' he said.

I wanted him to chuck his mate out and come to bed, but I could see by the way he kept licking his lips that he had taken some speed, so I knew there was no chance of that.

'I'm going to spend the night with Jody,' he said. 'Are you cool with that?'

I was taken aback and aware that the unknown man was listening to us. I knew Joe wanted us to have an 'open' relationship and I wasn't keen on this, but nothing had forced the issue until now.

'OK, I guess so,' I said with reluctance.

At that point I just wanted to be left alone with my clammy hot water bottle and cry. Joe left the room and the man continued to peer at me. I rallied and gritted my teeth and said, 'Do you think you could go somewhere else?'

He nodded and shuffled out of the room. I tried to go back to sleep but I was seething. I couldn't bear it any longer. I threw back the covers, shoved some clothes on and went off in search of Joe.

I found him in the living room. Things had not gone very far with Jody. Sitting side by side on a mattress holding hands, she was gazing at him with kohl rimmed doe eyes. Her skinny jeans and oversized jumper made her look even more waif like. I felt huge beside her, huge and in pain and angry. I didn't blame her; it was Joe I was furious with. A frisson of excitement ran through the room when I entered. For all of their laid-back cool, the assembled company knew a drama when they saw one.

'What's up, babe?' Joe said. 'You said this was cool, didn't you?'

'Oh yes, it is cool,' I hissed. 'You spend the night with her but afterwards you don't come back to me.' I was quite pleased with that line. I had been muttering it under my breath as I came down the stairs. I didn't know which way this would go, but I was so livid that I was prepared for the worst. If he wanted to shack up with his child bride so be it. I didn't give a fuck.

'Now calm down. You said this would be cool, didn't you?' Joe said, over and over again. I shrugged my shoulders.

'Your choice,' I said and looked at the young girl with pity.

'Good luck,' I told her, turned on my heel and marched upstairs. I had a sense that I had burnt my bridges but didn't care.

I flounced back into bed and shuffled about, trying to ignore the pain in my stomach that had receded during the drama but was now keeping me from sleep.

After a short while I heard footsteps on the stairs and sensed Joe coming into the room. With much sighing and rustling, he undressed and got into bed. I lay there as stony and cold as a marble statue. He was quiet, as though he was about to speak or he wanted me to speak, but I couldn't find any words and eventually neither could he. I felt as though I had been one step away from bad things but now they were finally catching up with me.

We never spoke about this again.

Soon after that night, the house on Sainsbury Road opened up and we moved once more.

Chapter Nine

The day we moved in someone slipped a hand-drawn flyer under our door: 'This Saturday come to Lloyd's Night of Love'. It was in all capitals on bright purple paper in bubble writing. Lloyd lived next door to us.

'That looks cool,' Joe said and shouted up to Donny and Dawn who were struggling with a mattress on the stairs. We met them at the pub just before we moved. He was a Scottish bloke and she was his London girlfriend. We liked them straight way and asked them to move in.

They let go of the mattress.

'Any excuse to skive, Donny,' sniped Dawn, and joined us in the kitchen for our first cup of tea.

Joe was wincing and cradling his hand which was wrapped in a damp and dirty tea towel. After hot-wiring the electrics, he had put his hand on one of the burners not realizing it was on and got a nasty burn.

'What's all this about?' he said showing the flyer to Donny. Donny had dark hair in a glam rock feather cut and sported a Zapata moustache. He had the most flared jeans I had seen for a while.

'Oh, aye. That's one of those blues nights,' he said.

Joe and I looked bewildered, and Donny's smile widened. He liked the chance to show off a little local knowledge to Londoners who thought they knew everything.

'Yes,' he said with a world-weary air. 'You pay the dude on the door some bread and then go in and buy drink and spliff. It's like a party that you pay to go to. But the music will be cool, and it's a great Saturday night out.'

Joe went next door to tell Lloyd we would be there and managed to wangle free entrance for all of us.

'He wants to keep on our good side, I think. He said it might be a little bit noisy.'

That was an understatement.

Lloyd opened the door and waved us through as we stepped into a sea of hot steamy plastic. Strips of it led us from the front door to the living room and then on to other parts of the house. His sofa was also protected by plastic. I sat on it and braced myself with my feet to avoid slipping off.

We bought cans of Breaker, a strong malt lager like Special Brew, and settled in — shouting at each other over the music. Sitting next to me was an older woman, obscured by a cloud of pungent smoke, our neighbour from the other side. She was on friendly terms with Lloyd and kept calling to him, trading insults in fast Jamaican patois that I couldn't understand. I caught her eye and she winked at me and gave me a nearly toothless grin. I found out her name was Edna and she had a lucrative sideline dealing small pound bags of home-grown grass cultivated in her back garden. In the weeks to come, Donny would often sit in our living room and pound on the adjoining wall wailing, after a particularly heavy dope session, 'Edna Edna what have you done to my heid?'

Luckily for our eardrums, and for the framework of the houses, Lloyd's Night of Love was an irregular event. I think he was wary of the police and local attention if he overstepped the mark and ran them too often.

Around the same time, other blues nights started happening in Crystal Palace too. Originating from Jamaican dancehall culture, the ones we went to seemed multi-racial and friendly towards a bunch of ragamuffin white kids. We paid our money and listened to great reggae music that we wouldn't hear anywhere else.

One night Jacob and Joe wanted to score, but Lloyd and Edna didn't have anything.

'Tell you what, we'll go down to the frontline and get some,' Lloyd said and drove the boys down to Railton Road in Brixton. Joe was nervous, and so was Jacob who was generally fearless. Lloyd tried to reassure them. 'It's just like the ones up the hill. That cool man, your money's as good as anyone else's. We'll have a drink and a smoke, it'll be good.'

The guy on the door took their money but as soon as they walked in it was obvious this wasn't like the ones they had been to before. It was hardcore and clear that their presence wasn't welcomed. Lloyd got lots of stick for bringing them. Fortunately, the boys' gift of gab smoothed the situation over and got them back in one piece. Although without any dope and having spent their stash on breakers and entrance.

'I bought two cans and didn't feel like I could ask for change,' Joe said.

* * *

Tessa moved into Sainsbury Road with us.

'It was too soon with Johnny. We're still going out but living together isn't working for us,' she said.

81

She moved into what would have been the dining room on the ground floor behind the living room and next to the kitchen. The toilet was outside and at the end of the garden, which was annoying for all of us.

We celebrated Christmas in our new house and to my surprise my mum, brother, and my stepfather Monty invited themselves over for Boxing Day. My mum sat on the sofa with Lloyd and various local n'er do wells who were away from their families. She looked chic next to our scruffiness — a black polo neck, a brightly coloured beaded necklace, and jeans rolled up to show her black boots. I think she had dressed down, but she outshone everyone there.

There weren't many squats in the area, but a small crowd had opened up an old factory and called it 'The Peanut Factory'. When they moved in there were sacks of peanuts on the floor and the name stuck.

In the warehouse area, they erected a teepee and were living in it. We had invited them round for Boxing Day and they brought an annoying curly-haired bloke who never stopped talking and I suspected was hyped up on sulphate.

They were on the sofa entertaining my mother and Monty was in the kitchen engaged in deep conversation with Jacob. My brother drank quietly straight from a bottle of some kind of bubbly (underage but it was Christmas). We were all having a great time, and the little Victorian terrace started to feel like home in a way that the other houses hadn't. My mum was appalled at the outside toilet though.

'Makes me feel like the war years,' she said and screamed at the lack of hot water. She made me promise to come 'home' for a bath regularly.

She was always someone who liked to be at the vanguard of anything new and I think she was coming round to the idea of me living this strange alternative squatter life.

Donny and Dawn got on well with my family. Donny had the kind of sharp Scottish humour that my mother loved, and they were both born in Glasgow so had a chat about places they knew.

Jacob disappeared and returned with Tina and her baby. The little girl was a great hit with my mother who jiggled her up and down on her knee and let her play with her beads.

'Do you know what that girl does for a living?' my mum asked when I was washing mugs in the kitchen.

'Yes, she's a dancer,' I said. 'Ballet I think.'

'Hmm, something not right there,' Mum said and went off to ferret it out.

'Good luck with that,' I thought, knowing how vague Tina could be.

To my surprise, Mum came back and said, 'I knew it. She's a stripper! Dancer indeed. I smelt a rat there I can tell you, too short for ballet anyway.'

I looked at her, astonished.

Then she told me about a club in Soho she used to go to with my dad where he'd meet other musos and have a jam. They'd be there all night and leave at dawn. Then she sighed and her eyes got misty. I loved hearing these snippets about my jazz musician father but was distracted at the Tina news.

'I can't believe I was so sure about the ballet,' I said. Mum laughed and tapped the side of her nose.

'Well, I knew. Seems a shame with that little girl, her husband seems OK though. Quite tasty as well if he got rid of that beard and smartened up,' she said and gazed at Jacob.

Monty came up to Joe and I.

'Well, we spent Christmas day in the home of a millionaire!'

(He was prone to exaggeration)

'With the finest food and wine, gold-plated taps in the bathroom and everything. BUT...'

(He paused for emphasis)

'There wasn't half the good atmosphere like there has been here. Thoroughly enjoyed myself, and it was good to have a conversation with someone intelligent,' he said and nodded at Jacob.

'Bloody hell, what am I? Chopped liver?' I said.

After that dramatic speech he decided that he'd had enough and rounded up Mum and my brother to drive home — over the limit probably, but he didn't care.

'Lovely Christmas!' shouted Mum at everyone as she was dragged out.

'See ya, Mont,' Jacob said, waving at his new pal.

My brother smiled. I think he had been going round drinking everyone's leftovers. But it had been nice to bring my very different worlds together for a day.

* * *

Jacob lived with his wife Tina, their baby, and two other blokes in a squat a few doors away from us. One was called Virgil, for reasons unknown to me, and the other was Ted. They were a volatile household, always having rows and shouting. Joe spent a lot of time there when I was at work, drinking and smoking with Jacob. The first time he met Ted didn't go well.

'Jacob and Tina's room is at the top and the bog is at the bottom of the garden like ours,' he said.

I thought I knew where this was heading.

'So, we were chatting and I couldn't be arsed to go to the bog and it was dark and rainy so I just pissed out the window. Usually that would be OK, but their kitchen has that weird lean to. Ted was in there making his dinner. There's a hole in the plastic of the lean to and it went all over him.'

We both laughed — Joe a little shamefaced.

'What did he do?'

'He went mental! He came upstairs shouting and carrying on. It wasn't helped that Jacob and me were laughing but it did seem funny at the time.'

'Oh Joe!'

'I know it can't have been nice getting piss all over your head and in your dinner,' Joe said, still sniggering.

'But I did say sorry. And I offered to go down to the chippy and get him some chips.'

'That was big of you, poor bugger.'

I felt sorry for Ted and wanted to like him. But when I first met him, I didn't take to him. He had a massive chip on his shoulder about being born in Penge of all things.'

'If I had been born in Upper,' he said, emphasising the word, 'Norwood like you—'

'I was born in Clapham,' I said, correcting him.

'Then I would have passed the eleven plus and my life would have been very different.'

'But I passed the eleven plus and I'm living in a squat and working in a pub.'

'Yes, but you don't have to.'

'I must be the only person I know who actually has a job,' I replied. 'There's no jobs around! Everyone's on the rock and roll, aren't they?'

I liked Virgil. He was the original rough diamond. Joe described him as a 'market trader without a stall'. That was

85

accurate, and probably why I liked him as it was my family background. He was an East End cockney who could look at you and make everything he said sound suggestive.

'Any chance of a cup of tea?' he would say, and I felt like we were going upstairs to the bedroom. He had a massive crush on Tessa and was always trying to get her to go off somewhere. But she was in love with Johnny and stayed true to him.

Virgil got on well with Joe so whether it was loyalty to him or that he just didn't fancy me I don't know, but I was quite attracted to him.

With dirty blond hair and bright blue eyes, he often wore a pork pie hat and an old man's tweed suit. An interesting look when most of the blokes I knew wore old jeans and a T-shirt or jumper. Joe was an exception with his adventurous choice of clothing — he sometimes would borrow dresses from me and Tessa and had a pale blue cord jumpsuit that he made himself and wore out.

I liked the idea of having Joe as my boyfriend and living with him more than the reality of a relationship. I had no idea how to behave in a partnership. I hadn't had it modeled to me by my mum and Monty who rowed continuously. Old romantic films obsessed my mum and I had been brought up on them.

'Oh, isn't that lovely,' she would say and sigh as Doris Day (who she resembled) and Rock Hudson fell into each other's arms. Then she'd say, 'How wonderful' at the end when the heroine finally met her dream man and the future was unknown but rose tinted.

I think she must have had this dream world in mind when she met my dad. He was a musician; the glamour of his TV gigs and after-hours parties in Soho with celebrities buoyed them along for a while. But after I was born the reality of living with someone who was on the road and in the bar leaving her at home with a small baby began to dawn on her.

'We came third after music and booze,' she would say. Monty seemed to represent a more stable life.

In the absence of any other role models, I took her celluloid ideals as mine, and some of the time I lived in the fantasy I had inhabited since childhood. I didn't have Rock Hudson; I started with Paul Newman and then pop music kicked in and finally Paul Weller replaced Marc Bolan. I never wondered if the unknown future, the dot dot dot after the film ended, the reality of day-to-day living would affect the romance of whoever I wanted to be with.

When I saw myself with one of these famous artists in my daydreams, I always viewed it from the outside, how great we would look to the people who saw us, and some of that carried on with my relationship with Joe. We didn't row or fall out and life bowled us along. We lived our lives in public, and as time went on, we became something of a star couple that had stayed together for a long time, especially by the standards of the people around us who changed partners constantly.

That winter in Sainsbury Road I carried on working in the pub, and Joe continued to be on the dole and drinking fruit wine in the day with his cronies. Many of the houses around us were empty or emptying, and he went in and out of them to scavenge things had been left behind. He didn't damage them, just scrounged around for the odd vase or ornament and took it up to the second hand and pawnshop at the top of the hill. My mum called the bloke who ran it 'Golden Balls' — she was great with nicknames — and he would buy any old tat Joe could find as it was extra fag and dope money.

We went to Saturday jumble sales for clothes and skips for furniture and got the cheapest food we could. I was allowed to take any uneaten rolls or sarnies from the pub at the end of my shift. Gathering in each other's houses didn't cost anything, and there were always the cheap Mondays in my pub for an outing. Occasionally we would have an Indian takeaway from the Asia Garden, but I didn't feel hard done by at all. I didn't pay rent and I lived with my friends — that's what was important to me rather than holidays or possessions.

One afternoon I was at Jacob's, and they had all been taking speed and were talking nineteen to the dozen. Tina and baby were asleep upstairs and Ted was holding forth to Joe and Jacob again about how life was so unfair to him and all of the things he could have done.

'Yeah, I was really interested in being a doctor, you know? I think I could've had a crack at that,' he said.

'Well, you know all about chemicals and dosage,' Joe said.

Virgil sat next to me and started to tell a long story about someone he used to go out with called Pat. I had never seen him with anyone, despite the continual suggestive talking and crush on Tessa, so I was intrigued by this insight.

'She worked in a circus and said she could get me in to watch her. It was on Clapham Common and was a pissy cold night,' he said and stopped to take a deep drag on his fag.

I noticed his old man's suit and checked shirt and kipper tie, in lurid colours, all looked like it hadn't been washed for a while; and the tie had a stain on it, possibly egg.

'She lifted up the side of the big top and I crawled in,' he said and looked at a place above my head, remembering. 'Inside the tent was warm and full of colour, all the shades you could imagine. It was like stepping out of a black and white film into Technicolor, like *The Wizard of Oz*.'

I was a bit taken back at this cultural reference, a side of Virgil I hadn't expected.

'There were animals, clowns, a ringleader, popcorn — and families, kids and parents, having a wonderful time enjoying themselves. Everyone laughing. Fucking magical it was,' he said and paused again, this time for a slurp of fruit wine. 'Anyway, I found a place to sit on a bench near the front, and I watched her on the trapeze. She had long red curly hair that flew behind her, and she wore a little thing — what do you call it?'

'Tutu?' I said.

'Yeah, one of those. Pink with shiny bits on it.'

'Sequins?'

He shrugged, impatient, drumming his fingers, speed movements.

'I dunno, maybe. She had those tights on with holes in them.'

In my head I thought 'fishnets' but didn't say anything this time.

'Anyway, she had a smile so wide and flew up higher and higher on her swing and kept catching my eye as she came down. You know, I really felt that she was doing it all for me. Everyone clapped after the act, but really it was just her and me and the lights and warmth — amazing.'

He had gone misty-eyed telling me this story and I was touched to have shared what was obviously a precious memory.

'Oh Virgil, how wonderful that sounds,' I said.

His blue eyes looked into mine and then down to the floor.

'Yeah, it's a pity she was such a slag.'

Chapter Ten

We didn't always stay in Crystal Palace. Occasionally we would venture further out. Soon after Christmas, in that strange time between Xmas and New Years, I had the day off and we went up West to Soho and Chinatown. Tessa and I were in search of little Kung Foo slippers, like Tina wore, that were cheap. Joe and Jacob were just along for the craic.

We got some cans of beer from an offy in Gerrard Street and the boys settled themselves outside a restaurant, sitting on the pavement, Tessa and I scoured the shops, having a great time looking at all of the unusual food and nipping back occasionally for a quick swig with Joe and Jacob.

I took a photo of the three of them leaning up against the shop window just as we were getting ready to leave.

'Hurry up, babe, my arse is frozen. I'm going to stick to this in a minute,' Joe said and blew smoke out into the dark frosty air.

'OK, we'll just try one more shop and then call it a day. Can't find the shoes anywhere.'

The owner of the restaurant came out and started shouting at us. We couldn't really understand him well, but it seemed that he thought we were putting customers off. Joe stood up and advanced towards him, hands down, placating.

'Sorry, man, we'll go in a minute. It's all cool,' Joe said. He was much taller than the shopkeeper and I think the little guy was worried that Joe was going to have a go at him. So he stepped back, but carried on shouting at us. We could recognise a few words.

'Whore, tramp, beggar, fuck off.'

Tessa started to get cross and said, 'Who do you think you're calling a whore? We're going in a minute, just give us a chance to get our stuff together.'

I stood behind her.

'Yeah and stop shouting — there's no need.'

He continued, and a small crowd gathered, interested to see what would happen.

'Well, you're really putting people off now, aren't you?' Joe said.

Jacob was excited. He loved drama like this and had had just enough beer to loosen him up. He moved towards the shouting shopkeeper.

'Look, mate, we've had enough. This is the Queen's highway, and we have every right to be here, so just push off my good man and we'll be on our way.'

Someone in the crowd laughed and I did snicker. Even though Jacob sounded unbearably pompous, he was funny.

That laughter was enough for the shopkeeper and tipped him over the edge. He took a swing at Jacob and Jacob, delighted, took a swing back and made contact, just with his arm. I didn't think the guy was hurt but Joe stepped in to try and break them up and there was a melee of arms and legs and shouting.

At that moment the police arrived with a van and screeched to a halt outside the shop. Two coppers jumped out and hauled the fighting human mess apart into three components, all breathing heavily and annoyed.

'What the fuck's going on here then?' said one of them, nodding at the shopkeeper. They all started talking at once. Jacob going on about the Queen's highway again. The crowd dispersed.

'What do you think?' said one copper to the other. 'Is it worth it?'

'Oh, fuck it, we've come out. Chuck them in. Him and the hippies. I've just had the van washed as well — smelly long-haired twats.'

To our horror they shoved all three men into the van then one copper got in with them and one got in the driver's seat. It all happened so quickly I didn't have time to react. The van's doors closed, the engine started, and it moved. I ran alongside it with Tessa, and we banged hard on the metal, peering into the wired window. It came to a halt and the back door flung open, making us both start back.

'Stop that, you silly bitches,' the one in the back shouted. 'Unless you want to come in as well.'

I could see Joe shaking his head and it did seem stupid for us all to be locked up, so I backed off.

'Where are you taking them?' I shouted.

'The local nick, darling,' he said, curled his lip, banged the door shut, and off they went. In despair, I watched as the taillights disappeared.

Then I turned to Tessa and said, 'Do you know where that is?'

She shook her head. I shivered. It was nighttime and getting cold and damp. The lights and bustle of Soho, the smells of roasting duck, all seemed so exciting and exotic a moment before. It now appeared strange and threatening and everything felt cheerless. A misty light rain started to fall.

We clutched each other, finding solace and warmth. A passerby who must have witnessed the exchange, came up to us. He was so muffled up with a hat and scarf that I could only see his eyes and a slit of mouth.

'Holborn, that's where they would have taken them, love.'

It took us a while to get there because we didn't know that part of London that well. It was getting late and colder.

'At this rate we'll miss the last bus home,' Tessa said, then asked yet another passerby for directions, another one who looked at us suspiciously and shook her head.

In the end we found the perfect solution — ask a policeman. He pointed us in the right direction, and we stumbled up the steps and in the front door.

'What do you want?' the bloke on reception said. He was curt but not unkind and confirmed that Joe and Jacob were both there. Then he told us to wait. We raided the machine for chocolate and settled in, every now and then asking him again what was going on. We hoped that by draping ourselves over the one hard wooden bench, making noise and being general pests, we would speed the process up. It was not to be. As the evening continued, drunks were bought in, arguing and shouting, and then manhandled somewhere beyond the entrance.

That was the only distraction. Otherwise it was boring and tedious and not unlike waiting in a hospital. We ran out of energy and chat and just sat there, dozing on the bench, scarred with initials and marks carved into it. After a couple of hours Joe came out.

'Where's Jacob?' I said. His face was grey with exhaustion and his hands hung at his side.

'Dunno,' he said. 'Don't ask me anything for a bit. I just want to get away from this shithole.'

We stumbled outside and down the dark streets, sparkling with dew from the damp air.

'What happened?' I asked after we had found a bus home.

'They wouldn't let me have a snout,' he said. 'We were so close to being just let off. They were arguing whether it was worth the paperwork. But I don't know, I just think they didn't like me, so they decided that it was worth it. I think it's the accent. It just turns people against me. They were SPG you know, Special Police Group, vicious fuckers.'

'Go on,' Tessa said.

She was kneeling on the seat in front of us, lurching as the bus heaved and stopped. Her knuckles gripped the metal bar, white and red from the cold. Condensation ran down the windows and a nice warm fug built up — the smell of fags, oil, people, and diesel making me warm and sleepy. Joe put his arm round me and nuzzled into me.

'What happened to the shop guy?' I said.

'Oh, he, the little fucker, got let out as they went round the corner. He bunged them, they must have an agreement with him as a regular. He had it on his toes.'

We all snorted in indignation at the unfairness of this, but more was to come.

'I've been charged,' Joe said.

'What with?' I shouted.

'Possession.'

'Fuck, I didn't know you were carrying,' Tessa said.

'Do you think I'm an idiot?' Joe said and banged his hand on the steel rail. 'I didn't have anything! I wouldn't go up town with anything.'

I felt bad but had to ask.

'Are you sure, Joe? Not something you forgot in a pocket?'

He turned to me, eyes wide.

'I'd tell you, honest, why wouldn't I? No, they were arguing about what to do and I was arguing back at them.'

My heart sank.

'Then one of them got out a little plastic bag with a lump of hash in it and grinned at me and said, 'Who's been a naughty boy then?'

We all sat in silence.

'So that's it then,' I said, close to tears. 'Will you have to go to prison?' I was wondering how I would manage without him.

'I don't think it'll come to that,' he said.

'Just don't say anything in court,' Tessa said and Joe gave her a dirty look.

When we got back we found Jacob in the living room with a few celebratory cans of Breakers and a joint.

'I was let out about the same time as you. But they let me out round the back so we wouldn't be together.'

They hadn't charged him, bastards.

Joe got notice of his court case within a week. It was at The Old Bailey in the middle of January, and I took the day off work to go up with him. He hadn't bothered to dress any differently.

'Doesn't seem any point really,' he said and just wore the usual jeans and jumper.

He had been advised by everyone to plead guilty to avoid a custodial sentence. At the entrance he was taken away. I looked up at the huge reception and went up the steps. I sat in the visitors' seats feeling alone and upset. Joe came up in the dock and I let out a squawk. Then he turned around and smiled as an usher glared at me. It was over very quickly; he pleaded guilty. One of the arresting officers read out a statement.

'Lies, lies, lies, lies was all I heard. It bore no relation to what actually happened.'

I left and went outside to wait. Joe came down the steps looking rueful. He had a fine that he intended to pay by borrowing off his parents.

'What will they say?' I said.

'Oh, they won't be surprised. They gave up on me a long time ago.'

I squeezed his arm and we walked through all of the city gents with bowler hats and umbrellas.

He was given a hero's welcome when we got home. I think Jacob was feeling relieved and a little guilty.

'You took the rap for me, man,' he kept saying, hugging Joe. 'I think they let me off because I had a kid and all.'

He had stumped up for chips all round and more cans of beer, so we had a celebratory dinner with Don, Dawn, and Tessa. Ted appeared towards the end and hoovered up the leftovers.

'You're a champion,' he said clapping Joe on the back, their previous enmity forgotten. 'You do it for the people,' he bellowed with more clapping.

I could see Joe wincing; Ted was a meaty guy and Joe was not.

'Yeah, alright working-class hero. Help me carry these plates out to the kitchen and wash up,' Tessa said.

'It did feel scary,' I said to Joe later. 'I didn't know what I'd do if you had been put away.'

'Oh, you'd be fine,' he said, half asleep.

I didn't know if I would be. I hadn't made it to uni because I had panic attacks if I was travelling on my own, and for a while I didn't want to go outside of my familiar Crystal Palace world, even with someone. I was better now and could travel with friends, but still refused to go on a plane or the tube. Outwardly I appeared confident and was good with people, hence my work in the pub. Underneath I often felt anxious, and the thought of being adrift without Joe took me to a dark place. I wondered if that was what was keeping us together, but I didn't want to examine this too closely.

I had seen little of Tina. Joe, who was closer to Jacob because of the afternoon drinking sessions, told me they weren't getting on that well. Tina was fed up living with three blokes and the place was a tip. Even Joe didn't think it was suitable for a child, so Jacob opened up another deserted house for Tina and baby and helped them get it in some kind of shape to live in with electrics and basic furniture. They didn't live there together.

I went round one day to see how she was and found her sitting in her living room with her child who was wearing one of her T-shirts and smelt like she had a full nappy. She was pulling herself up on the little table in the middle of the sparsely furnished room.

'She'll be walking soon,' I said, surprised at how much progress the little one had made. I offered to make tea and while I was waiting for the kettle to boil, I did a little washing up and tidying in the kitchen. I had brought round a packet of biscuits as a moving in present. Tina opened them and gave the child one. She seemed a little despondent, the spark that she used to have wasn't there.

'I've lost my job. I kept taking time off to look after bubs because Jacob was too out of it so they fired me,' Tina said.

'What are you going to do?'

She shrugged and did a little pout.

'Fuck knows. Sign on, I guess. I can't go looking for dance work if I have a child with me. Club owners don't like it.'

I was always fascinated by Tina. She was so tiny and had a little spiky elfin haircut that she said she did herself. I was tempted to get her to do mine the same way. I had gone a bit shorter but was nervous about a full chop. Everything inside me was urging my mouth to open and say that I would look after her baby. I had such a strong desire to help Tina, to help anyone, I was a born problem solver.

Ultimately, I knew that she would take advantage of me, so I metaphorically bit my tongue. There was silence between us, and I think Tina expected me to offer. I had a brainwave.

'You could ask Dawn. She works part time at a café and might have the odd morning off.'

I didn't know if this was true or not. I did know that Dawn adored babies and was desperate to have children of her own. She was always pestering Donny, the thin interior walls of the house meant we had little privacy, so I heard it all. Dawn was much more maternal than I was, and I comforted myself with that thought. Tina's face lit up.

'Oh, what a great idea. I'll nip round and ask her,' she said. Then she gestured at the baby who was gnawing on the table and said, 'Would you?'

'Yes, of course I will,' I said and realised the trap I had walked myself into.

Tina put on her little Chinese slippers, the ones that Tessa and I wanted to buy, and tripped off. I played pee boo with the little one for what seemed like hours, gave her another biscuit and a drink of water, changed her nappy, and put her on my hip and had a poke around upstairs.

There wasn't much there. One bedroom was deserted, and the other just had a double mattress on the floor and a grubby looking carrycot next to it. There were two nails stuck into an alcove with string between them and various sparkly and gauzy things hung up. I was tempted to have a rummage through, but I was worried that Tina would catch me, so I scuttled back downstairs.

Finally, the baby seemed tired so I rocked her to sleep in my arms and then wedged her onto the mattress on the floor with a couple of pillows so she wouldn't roll off. I made myself some more tea, there was no more milk. Luckily, I had a library book in my bag so I settled down to read an old Marjorie Allingham mystery.

After a couple of hours Tina came back in a flurry. She woke the child who began to cry.

'Oh, my darling, have you missed your mama?' she said, picking the baby up and violently rocking her, murmuring something in Greek that I couldn't understand.

'I hope she hasn't slept all this time, has she? You might not know as you don't have experience, but if you let them sleep too much in the day they won't sleep at night.'

'Bloody cheek,' I thought and said huffily, 'I practically brought up my younger brother.' I was stretching the truth a little, but still.

'Did you find Dawn?' I said.

Tina looked at me with wide eyes, she had obviously forgotten the whole purpose of the trip.

'Oh her,' she said waving her hands vaguely. 'She wasn't in so I had to see Jacob.'

She called him 'Yaacob'.

'Then I went to the top of the hill to look at the view.'

Her baby had been put down and now, unnoticed by her mother, crawled towards the fireplace, and started rummaging in the burnt bits of wood, covering herself in soot. I was on my high horse and didn't want to help. Instead, I got up and got my

99

things ready to leave. Tina grasped my hands and looked into my eyes.

'I can't thank you enough,' she said. 'It was so nice to get out and walk about.'

I felt bad.

'You should get her,' I said, gesturing towards the mucky little one.

Tina gave a little whoop and pounced on her, laughing at the mess and following me into the hall.

'Now then, say thanks to your aunty,' she said, making me feel even worse with her gratitude after my uncharitable thoughts about her. I tried to make it up to her as we stood on the doorstep.

'It was lovely seeing you,' I said.

One of the few original tenants came out at the same time and gave us a sour look. Tina waved at her brightly.

'Hello, dear,' she said to the elderly woman who ignored us and slammed the door behind her.

'I'll see you soon,' I said to Tina, holding the baby's little foot. 'I'll pop round again.'

'Anytime,' Tina said and went back inside. I had a moment of feeling broody; they seemed so happy. I wondered what would happen to them, if their little family would make it through.

Chapter Eleven

One afternoon, I came home from work to find Joe and Tessa sitting in silence in the kitchen. They looked up as I came in.

'I've got some cheap slightly stale cake from the Polish bakery,' I said putting it on the side and lighting a match under the kettle. 'Anyone fancy some toast made with Babka?'

There was no reply.

'You'd better tell her,' Tessa said.

I turned round holding a carving knife in my hand.

'What?'

Joe came over, took the knife away, and held my hand.

'You should sit down,' he said.

'Tell me quickly,' I blurted out. 'My mum, Adam?'

'No, it's Tina,' he said.

I sat down on the kitchen chair.

'But I just saw her the other day,' I said, tears starting to well. 'She was fine, what happened?'

'It was her heart,' Joe said. 'Jacob was here earlier; he's gone with his little one to stay with her sister. Tina's heart just gave out.'

'She was always a bit breathless,' Tessa said. 'I was worried about that and the speed. I think that's what did for her.'

'So, who found her?'

Tessa and Joe looked at each other. There was something else going on.

'It was Ted,' Tessa said. 'He went round there. She had given him a set of keys and he wanted to see her about money or something. There was no answer when he knocked so he looked through the letterbox and saw the baby on the floor crying. He used his keys and went in and found Tina in bed.'

'So, he called 999?' I said. 'There was no chance then? She had gone already?'

Again, they looked at each other.

'We've just heard this from Jacob,' Tess said. 'But apparently he didn't call the ambulance.'

'What?'

'No, he went back to the house and said to Jacob, "Tina's dead and we need to split because the cops are coming and I sold her speed."'

We all sat in silence.

'What a bastard,' I said. 'Maybe she could have been saved if he'd called them instead of thinking about saving his own skin.'

'We don't know that, babe,' Joe said.

'I agree with Deb,' Tessa said. 'Fucking selfish bastard. I can't think of that poor child, sitting there with her mother for God knows how long. I think he just left her there while he went round to tell Jacob.'

'Jacob called the ambulance, then old Bill came. He ran round and picked up the little one and then had to identify Tina. Tomorrow her folks are coming to pick up her stuff. Jacob said he doesn't want to stay at Tina's sister's with the baby too long as she'll try and take her away from him.'

'Would that be such a bad thing?' Tessa said.

I nodded in agreement.

Joe shook his head and flicked the end of his cigarette into the sink.

'I dunno, she is his kid.'

Tessa and I looked at each other.

This meant that Jacob's house would be empty as well as Tina's. With Jacob and his kid gone, Ted skived off and Matt, I didn't know about Matt.

'What will Matt do with Jacob gone?' I said.

Joe raised his eyebrows and shrugged. He was moving around the kitchen, opening tins and making a pasta sauce. The smell of frying onions and garlic filled the air.

'He'll probably go back up the road home,' Tessa said.

We sat round that evening eating pasta with sauce and grated cheese sharing memories of Tina. Tessa had a bottle of actual wine, rather than the cheap fruit stuff, and we raised our glasses.

'I tried to get retsina, you know because she was Greek, but they didn't sell it,' she said.

'I can never forgive Ted,' I said, another person to add to my hit list.

'Well, he didn't force her to take speed. If it hadn't been him it would have been someone else,' Joe said.

'She shouldn't have taken it with a dicky heart,' Tessa said.

We stayed in the kitchen; the cooking had made it nice and warm and I shivered thinking of our cold bedroom. I kept wondering if there was something I could have done, some way I could have helped Tina more.

Dawn and Donny came back from the pub. They had bumped into Matt at Gypsy Hill station. As predicted, he had a bag with him and was going back up to Scotland.

'He didn't know where Ted had fucked off to,' Donny said, his mouth screwed up like he was going to spit but thought better of it.

'What a shit, and that poor little girl,' Dawn said, her eyes filling with tears. Donny patted her arm.

'Never mind, hen. She'll be well looked after by Jacob's sister.'

'He's always dumping her on his sister.'

Dawn didn't belong to Jacob's fan club, and Tessa and I had given up membership after living at close quarters with him and seeing his neglect of Tina and his child.

'This time he should leave her there.'

* * *

Tina's death left a gap in our squat family as two houses were now empty. Life seemed to carry on as normal but every now and then I felt her ghostly presence and it made me shiver.

As traumatic as Tina's death had been, it wasn't the only death I experienced at Sainsbury Road. The next one would have far reaching consequences beyond our squat community.

One night a few weeks later, Joe and Donny had gone off to score. Dawn was at her mum's and I had the evening off work. Tessa and I decided to go out.

'And we're coming back after those blokes,' she said.

We did a pub-crawl round Crystal Palace. It was a quiet night and after a few drinks we decided it wasn't worth staying out just to spite the boys, so we came back home. As we approached our house, I saw a car idling outside. It was an unusual sight as the road wasn't a through road and cars generally only came down when they were visiting. Not many people I knew had a car.

'Aye aye, what's up?' Tessa said.

I saw a lean figure propped against the car smoking a fag and recognised who it was, a friend of my mother's and Monty's called Ron.

'Finally,' he said, peeling himself off the car and walking towards us.

'Is everything OK?' I said.

'No, it's not. I've been sent to get you,' he said and hesitated. 'It's Monty.'

He didn't need to say more. My stepfather was asthmatic and had had two heart attacks. One of them in the late 60s when we had all driven to Morocco and lived on the beach for a few months. He had the attack just outside Granada in Spain on the journey home. We had stayed in a Catholic convent for a while as he was being nursed. The other one was in Tunisia on a family holiday. The attack happened as he jumped in the hotel pool and a student nurse helped him. He came to with his head lying on her knees, staring up at her breasts in a bikini.

'Am I in heaven?' he quipped. Monty always had an inhaler on him. If he ever forgot it then the lack of one was likely to bring an attack on.

'Is it bad?' I asked Ron.

'Very bad,' he said and put his hand on my shoulder. 'You'd better take some stuff for overnight; your mum needs you.'

My mother had finally left Monty. After years of rowing and bickering she had taken the plunge and moved in with a friend nearby. She left Adam with his dad. The Christmas at our house was their last outing together as a family.

Joe wasn't home yet. I wrote him a note and shoved some things into a plastic carrier bag. I was running on adrenalin and pushing any emotions to the back of my mind — concentrating on practical matters as they were something I could cope with. Downstairs I saw Tessa, also with a bag.

'You're coming with me?' I asked her, surprised.

'Course I am, mate, come on.'

I sat in the back, not asking for any more details while we were driven to my old home. It wasn't far, just round the corner in Upper Norwood. When we got there the house was full of people who had all obviously been to the pub. My mum was in floods of tears which intensified when she saw us. It took a while to get the story out of her. Monty had gone to the local pub, the Beulah Spa, and had a drink there. He left at closing time, had a massive heart attack in his car and died. He was found when the landlord looked in the car park and got a dreadful shock. It was such a sad ending to his life.

I felt completely numb. My mother seemed to suck all available emotion out of the air leaving me with nothing to feel. I hadn't always got on well with Monty, but he had been part of my life since I was a small child. I felt that he didn't really know how to relate to a growing troubled girl and Adam was always his number one. However, that didn't drive a wedge between Adam and I. Being the golden boy wasn't all it was cracked up to be. We both suffered with our parents' constant drunken rows and dramas.

Adam had been in the house on his own that evening when the police came round. They told him about his dad without my mum there. I was furious. He was only fifteen. He seemed dazed with exhaustion and shock and soon retreated to his room.

Late into the night we all sat and drank brandy and milk which helped me get to sleep in my old room in the double bed with Tessa snoring next to me. The next day was a blurred mess as well. Tessa left and Joe came to see how I was. There was a lot more brandy and milk and I phoned the pub to get a few days off work. Family members started to visit and my mum moved her stuff back in. It was hard to get a sense of how my brother was as there was so much going on.

A week later, in the car on the way to the funeral, he wrote 'Arsenal' in steam on the back window. He looked round at me, thinking that he would be told off. I put my arm round him and kissed his head. We both sat in silence.

The ceremony at the crematorium was perfunctory. Monty was Jewish but not observant. He was estranged from some of his family and had been a Communist in his youth. The numbness I felt at his death continued. At the drunken wake in the house later, I looked round. We were all dressed in black, and I saw several people I knew he wouldn't have allowed in the house talking about him as though they had been great friends.

I felt so angry, but I didn't know what about or who it was directed at. My mother hadn't stopped sobbing and I didn't know if she felt guilty, grief-stricken, or was just drunk. I couldn't wait to get away from the mayhem and as soon as possible I left and got a bus home.

Standing at the top of Gypsy hill, it was a cold bright night, and I could see stars and London laid out before me with an amazing clear view. Suddenly I started to cry. There was so much I would have liked to ask him and now it was too late.

Chapter Twelve

Tina and Monty's deaths had shaken everyone, not just my family. All of the housemates had met my mum and Monty at Christmas. Tessa had known him from a very young age.

'Do you remember when you said we had to have a midnight feast? And you scuttled upstairs with biscuits leaving me to face Monty in his dressing gown wanting to see where all the noise was coming from?'

'I think I had read too much *Mallory Towers*,' I said.

'I remember after Honey we got a dog called Peanut. He was a stupid little white mutt and got very snappy. One day he was in the car with Monty and jumped on his head while he was driving. We had to get rid of him!' I said and we both laughed; it was good to tell these stories. We were on our way to a jumble sale.

We bumped into Rosy and Gerry who were going to the same jumble sale and we walked together. It was odd, I thought, when we lived in Farquhar Road together we saw each other all the time but another house, another collection of mates.

'Have you heard?' Gerry said. 'We're being rehoused.'

'How's that happening?'

'Farquhar Road is just into Southwark. The council wants the house back to do it up and let it out. They've said that we can all get places that are hard to let. Gaffs that no one else wants basically.'

'Do you know where?'

Rosy looked a bit glum.

'That's the hassle. Because it's Southwark, that's where it'll be. Could be anywhere. It's a big borough. They give you one choice and that's it. You have to take it or nothing,' Rosy said.

Gerry tucked his hand in her arm. They were about the same size, like little people who came out of a cuckoo clock. I was glad to see that Ringo was still with them trailing behind. Tessa went to give him a cuddle.

'We're getting buses and travelling around to see the different areas,' Gerry said. 'It's quite an adventure! The house wasn't the same after you two left. It's time to move on and get somewhere proper.'

Rosy poked me and said, 'You should try and get one. You lived in the house.'

'How do I go about it?' I said.

We stopped outside the church hall where the jumble sale was. We were early and a queue was forming. We took our places and sat in line on a low wall.

'No dogs,' said a stern looking vicar hovering around.

'Oh, don't mind, mate, I'll wait outside with him. Rosy, see if you can get me some trousers, the arse is hanging out of these,' Gerry said.

There was tutting from the rest of the queue, mainly older women and one of them looked at him and said, 'Language.'

Gerry smiled and winked at her. She made a pursed cat's bottom mouth then turned her back to us. Rosy settled herself on the wall.

'It would be brill if you got a place near us, wouldn't it?' she said. 'You just have to show them a couple of bits of ID.'

'Hmm. No harm in checking it out,' I said.

Tessa gave me a sideways look but didn't say anything. Then the doors opened and we elbowed our way in. Rosy got some trousers for Gerry, they had braces attached to them and he was delighted with his new threads. Tessa found a great tweed coat, oversized like we had seen some girls wearing in the pub. On the walk home she was sniffing it suspiciously and then fished in the pocket and found an old bus pass showing the picture of a bewildered looking old man.

'Oh, I can't wear this now. I'd always be thinking of him, poor old bleeder,' she said.

'Don't be silly, he wouldn't have wanted it to go to waste.'

I held up my find. An orange beaded bolero jacket, probably 1920s.

'Oh, that's so cool,' Tessa said.

'Tina would have looked great in it,' I said and we looked at each other.

We got back and showed Joe our bargains (including a warm scarf for him). Then Tessa went to her room, and I told Joe all about the Farquhar Road scheme.

'Well, we like it here, don't we?' he countered.

'Yeees,' I said. 'But it would be nice to have our own place and an inside bog.'

'And hot water. Well, no harm in checking it out.'

I rustled up a library card and a doctor's card and sent them off to Southwark council not really expecting much.

Then a few things happened in quick succession that made me pin my hopes a bit more firmly on the possible Southwark hard to let. Tessa announced that she was going to have another crack at nurses training and would be living in halls in central London.

'I want to stick at it and qualify this time,' she said. 'I'll always be coming back here, and I can stay at Johnny's when I'm not working.'

The other thing that happened was I lost my job. The landlord and his drunken wife had been succeeded by a younger version of the same minus the psycho dog. There had been some financial shenanigans and the pub was losing money. The new landlord was emphatic that it was down to the cheap Mondays.

'We should never have carried those on,' he said as I polished glasses half listening to Chicago 'If You Leave Me Now' and wishing they had Elvis Costello on the jukebox.

'I could have made a go of this place if she,' he said, nodding towards his wife who was clutching onto the bar to balance on her stool, 'had stepped up a bit. Now if I had someone like you beside me...'

Here his voice got lower and more intimate. I glanced uneasily around, seeing if there was anyone to serve. Luckily a regular came in.

'Lager and lime, is it?' I said quickly pouring the drink.

The brewery had lost faith and was calling time on the whole setup. We were all getting our P45s and a small pay off and the landlord and his missus were bound for another, smaller pub as a last chance.

I was at home more and because of this I realised how much Dawn and Donny were rowing. They had always been a vociferous couple, but it seemed to have escalated. Dawn was fed up being the only one working, fed up with Donny's drinking, fed up being too embarrassed to take him to her mum's, and fed up with no plans for the future as she wanted stability and perhaps a baby. Donny was just fed up with her 'nagging'.

The shouting and occasional loud thuds against their bedroom door worried me. I liked Donny, he made me laugh, but as a boyfriend I thought he could be violent and had a short fuse. I had seen him in a temper and his black eyes sparkled with a light I didn't like. He seemed to turn from the genial joking guy to a coiled spring of fizzing bad energy. Their whole relationship seemed to have deteriorated and was spiraling out of control. When I bumped into Dawn in the kitchen, she seemed quiet and just scuttled in and out. I saw a purple mark that looked like a bruise on her arm.

Some strong speed had been doing the rounds and it had messed with his head, I thought. He was also bringing people, blokes, back to hang out in the living room and get high. Now that I was around more, I didn't like that. The room always smelt of testosterone and fags when they left, and I didn't like the look of them. They were friendly enough but sometimes when I left the room I heard them burst into laughter. I felt wary of this crowd.

I also wondered where Donny was getting the money to score. Joe didn't have Jacob to knock around with anymore, but he seemed reluctant to spend time with Donny and his mates which was unlike him.

When the letter came from Southwick council I was delighted and rushed to show Joe the good news.

'They're giving us a place!' I screamed. Joe was more cautious.

'Where is it?' he said.

I read further down and my face dropped a little. I knew realistically that we would have to leave the Palace but I was hoping that we would be just down the hill a bit, only slightly into Southwark. Joe took the letter off me.

'Peckham. Well, there's no harm in having a look.'

We got the 63 bus. It took ages and with every mile my fear intensified. I wasn't sure I would be able to do this journey alone. What would I do stuck out there away from my friends and family? I looked out the window at the unfamiliar streets and shops. Eventually we stopped and Joe tugged at my hand. He could see that I was upset but had no real understanding of the way that anxiety could grip and paralyse me. My heart was pounding and my hands were sweaty in his grasp.

'It's not far from the bus stop,' he said. 'And look, there's a cinema right by us!'

That did seem positive, and I produced a wan smile. The bloke from the council met us and showed us the flat. It was on the first floor in one of the traditional council low-rise red brick layouts that could be seen all over London. In each building an external pathway ran round and formed a square around the flats, with an internal courtyard for each block. I looked down over the low wall and saw a load of rubbish. There were washing lines where it was clear in the past it had been a pleasant patch of green. A place where neighbours met and children played and people looked out for each other. Now there were burnt out cars and heaps of old rusting fridges and bits of washing machines.

The council worker saw my look of horror and sighed.

'There's a reason they're hard to let,' he said. 'This isn't Dulwich.'

We carried on walking and he fished out a big bunch of keys. He let us into the flat. Indoors was better. The one-bedroom flat had been recently painted and smelled fresh. The windows looked onto the street behind which wasn't as scary as the courtyard. The bathroom was clean and had hot water. In the living room there was an electric bar fire and it felt warm and cosy.

'I'll leave you a minute,' he said and went outside where we could smell he was having a fag.

We both paced around and then met up in the living room. 'There's no cooker or fridge,' Joe said, loudly, directing it at the man. He stubbed his fag out and came back in, bringing the smoke with him.

'We'll give you both if you take it,' he said. 'Reconditioned ones.'

Joe looked at me and I shrugged. I needed time to have a think.

'OK, thanks,' Joe said. 'We'll give you a ring.'

'Don't take too long. We've got a list of people needing to be rehoused.'

We walked out to the road behind and looked up at where we thought our flat was.

'Sumner Road Estate,' Joe said. 'What do you think?'

I didn't know what I thought.

'Let's look around,' I said, pleased to be near an Odeon cinema and also a local park that seemed nice. My spirits started to lift and I tried to think about the newly painted interior and not the exterior of the flat.

On the bus home I looked out the window with more confidence. I could get a job doing something round here, I was sure. It all looked so bustling and full of people. Tessa would come and see me and my mum had a car — she'd come.

'If we took the flat, we'd be council tenants,' Joe said making a rollup and spitting bits of tobacco out as he licked the Rizla paper. 'Then after a while we could get a swap maybe.'

I nodded.

'Yes, as soon as we closed the door it would be our little place, wouldn't it?'

'It's that or nothing,' Joe said.

When we got back, we told Dawn and Donny what we were going to do. They were upset but I think quite pleased at the idea of having the house to themselves. That was Dawn's plan. Donny started to talk about having one of his mates in our room; I could see that she wasn't too keen on this. We phoned the council and started to pack. Joe knew someone with a van who could take our stuff to Peckham for a drink.

We didn't have a massive amount: a couple of mattresses, my old chest of drawers from home, some bookshelves, books, and then clothes and kitchen things. It had mainly been our stuff in the kitchen and I felt bad leaving Dawn with nothing (she did all of the domestic duties) but they had a cooker and a fridge as we were getting new ones.

The weekend before we left Winston had a Night of Love Blues, a great sendoff and also a reminder of why I wanted to leave. My mum was pleased that I would be paying rent and living in a proper flat. I had a job coming up in a month at the Ideal Homes Exhibition working for my uncle — my mum worked there also — and he needed someone else, so I asked Tessa who had some time off from her course.

We lasted a month in the Peckham flat. We found out the estate had the local name of 'Murder Mile'. There were constant fights, screaming, parties, and sirens sounding at all times. I was cautious about our neighbours. It felt a bit like junior school where I hadn't fitted in, as most of the kids knew each other from the local estate. My family were market traders and had working class credentials, but I had a Jewish stepfather. We lived in a big house, though it was rented. Somehow, we had a taint of the exotic that made the others view me with suspicion.

It was the same here all over again. The promised cooker and fridge didn't materialise and Joe made enterprising dinners using the electric fire. One night he spent ages doing this and then my mum turned up with fish and chips. I clung to him and stayed by his side so at times he got irritable with me and I'm sure felt trapped.

'I'm only nipping out to get fags,' he'd say.

The job at the IDH came up. Tessa and I spent a month selling dreadful art and candle kits. During that time we couldn't commute to Olympia so we stayed in a bed and breakfast where my uncle's workers stayed. The work was hard as the exhibition was open 9am — 9pm but we had a lot of fun and met some great characters.

There was an immortal moment at the very beginning when the exhibition was open to guests and celebrities before the general opening. Our stall was tucked away so we didn't always know what was going on or who was nearby. Tessa was walking around idly.

'Seems to be a big crowd heading this way,' she said.

'Who is it?' I said.

'Dunno, a load of blokes and some tiny woman in a pink hat,' she said and squinted a bit then looked at me in alarm. 'It's the queen mother, fuck me, what if she speaks to us?'

We started laughing hysterically and dived under the counter of the stall and stuffed our fists in our mouths. HRH came down with her entourage and stopped right outside our stall for ages. We were opposite a Ladbrokes stall, of interest to her. I thought I would burst and felt sick with hysteria.

On Saturday nights we could leave for a day as the exhibition was closed on Sunday. Tessa went back to Johnny's and I went to my mum's. Joe was staying in my childhood room while I was working. We had decided that at the end of the month, when the exhibition was finished, we would pool my wages and his dole and go to Greece. He was going to book us a passage on the Magic Bus. I was scared of flying.

Mum drove us to work on Mondays and I didn't see Joe until the next Saturday evening.

'Guess who I bumped into?' Joe said one Sunday morning.

'Who?'

'Jacob,' he said handing me a cup of tea.

Joe got into bed, settled himself against the pillows and continued.

'Yes, and he's married again.'

'What?!' I screamed.

Adam rushed in at the noise and it took a while to get him out. I couldn't wait to tell Tessa this nugget of news when I saw her the next day at work.

'Joe met her. She's French, very sweet, younger than him, and has long hair. They're living in a squat in Brixton. But he came to the Palace to see if anyone was around. He's got the baby back now. He's quite chubby as well,' I said to Tessa.

I couldn't believe it. Jacob always had a thin Lenny Bruce look about him, part of his attraction.

I carried on with Tessa selling the art and the candle making kits at the IDH. The guy demonstrating how to make the candles was an old hippy who lived nearby. A really nice guy who had us back one evening for dinner. Seeing him and his partner made me long for a home and domesticity as we were always eating takeaways, sandwiches, and strange fried breakfasts at the B & B.

The owners couldn't really deal with us being vegetarians.

'Here you are, girls,' the wife said. 'Call me Aunty Barb, everyone does.' The fried egg slipped across the plate where it had been sitting on top of tinned macaroni cheese.

We always went out in the evening and avoided the pub where the old-time grafters went and where my mum would be. We found another one with a younger crowd and bumped into a woman from junior school who now lived locally. It was a fun gang, and we were often drunk on the way home.

Tessa couldn't resist a skip.

'Look at that,' she'd say. 'Let's have a poke about.'

One night she insisted on dragging out a raffia rug and a road sign lamp that she made me carry back to the B & B.

'Anyone around?' she'd say, and I had to be on lookout.

'No, all quiet, sergeant.'

We struggled up the stairs and shoved the rug under the bed out of sight and the lamp in the corner, trying not to wake everyone with our laughter.

The next day after work our room was buzzing with flies.

'Fuck me Tess, that thing's alive!' I screamed and threw open the windows. 'Get it out, get it out!'

We shoved it into the empty room next door.

'Never again,' I said, shaking my fist.

On the last Sunday before the IDH closed I phoned home. It was one of the few times the phone wasn't cut off for nonpayment. Joe had more news. Jacob's new French wife had had enough and hot tailed back to Brittainy where her family were waiting with sympathy.

'They loved me when they met me at the wedding,' Jacob had said. 'But she told them all sorts about me.'

'Huh, probably most of it true,' I said to Joe.

'He's got someone else.'

'You're kidding me!' I cried. This was like a soap opera.

'Some girl from Peckham. I think it might just be someone to look after the baby from the way he was talking. He was making out that she's a nanny. Anyway, he wants to take over our flat when we've gone. That would work because our stuff would be safe.'

I hesitated. I had some nice bits and pieces that I had picked up over the years at jumble sales, some art deco pictures and ornaments.

'He said he'd wrap up the ornaments and stuff and put them away. It would save us having to organize everything and time is tight between you finishing work and us going to Greece.'

'OK, but make sure you tell him to be careful.'

Chapter Thirteen

The trip to Greece didn't start well. We got on the coach at Victoria and the Magic Bus rep counted everyone then sat down at the front. He was supposed to stay with us for the journey and see to passports and arrangements. When we got to Dover and were about to board the ferry he staggered over, shoved a load of paperwork at Joe and said, 'I can't go with you, man. I feel too crap. You take over, it'll be cool.'

Walking up the gangplank of the ferry gave me a jolt. We had got up so early that I was only now waking up. The journey so far had been a dream that I drifted through but now what I was doing finally struck me: I was leaving Britain without my family.

Everyone was drinking in the bar, excited at the novelty of getting drunk outside licencing hours. It felt like a school outing.

'What do you fancy?' Joe said, but the slight rolling and pitching of the ferry made me nauseous. I shook my head and left him. My ability to be sick on a car, plane or boat was the stuff of family legends.

'You were pea green,' my mum would say with a slightly proud air.

I felt panicked. Here there was no one older than me to slip me a pill, hold my hair while I threw up, or put a wet flannel on my head afterwards.

Through the heavy doors I found myself outside in a sea mist and staggered on the slippery deck in search of fresh air and the toilets.

'When do we get to Calais?' I asked a deckhand who was obviously used to the swaying movement. He looked at me bemused and said, 'Calais? Nah love, we're off to Zeebrugge.'

I couldn't help the shocked expression on my face. The ferry horn startled me, and I gripped his sleeve.

'Where's that? How long will it take?'

He shook me off, clearly thinking I was drunk.

'About seven hours, the usual,' he said and walked away.

Over the rails, the white cliffs start to fade away and I wanted to throw myself over and swim towards them. My lip started to tremble. I couldn't endure hours and hours of this, I just couldn't. The diesel fumes made my head ache. I gave myself a mental shake and swallowed. I had worked hard for this trip. I was the last of my friends to go away without their parents. I hadn't even been on a UK holiday without them.

A sudden gust of wind whipped up my cotton wraparound skirt. I clamped my hand down to avoid flashing my knickers and hobbled back into the bar. The pungent smell of beer and a cloud of smoke greeted me. I pushed my hair back off my face and found Joe in the middle of a crowd telling some long, involved story.

'Where did you go to, babe?' he said, patting the chair next to him.

'Felt a bit off.'

He studied my face.

'You do look a bit peaky,' he said, then introduced me to Aiden, a young bloke about our age who grinned, shook my hand, and passed me a bottle.

'Have some brandy, that'll sort you out. If it doesn't, I've got some Valium that'll do the trick.'

The brandy burnt on its way down but he was right, I did feel better.

I couldn't eat but managed to find a velvet sofa outside of a casino and fell asleep for a while. Joe and his new pals were still drinking when I left them, but when I woke up I found Joe with Aiden asleep on the floor at my feet. The ferry sounded different. It had a soft purr rather than a rumble.

I shook Joe's shoulder and said, 'I think we're there.'

'Fuck me, my head hurts,' he said, sitting up and scratching.

He gave Aiden a gentle kick.

'Wakey wakey, man,' he said.

Aiden sat up, smiling instantly.

'Time to find our coach.'

When we docked, Joe, in a drunken haze, still managed to find the crate with our luggage and eventually found our coach. This wasn't the Magic Bus experience we had been promised. Two cross, thickset blokes were in charge. It definitely wasn't the laid-back hippy vibe that was advertised. The drivers barked orders at us.

'No music and no drinking,' they said and confiscated Aiden's bottle of whiskey so we all hid our own stashes.

During the bumpy, three-day bus ride to Greece, I wrote letters to Tessa. My clothes stuck to me and I knew that I smelt.

You wouldn't want your flannel anywhere near my chukky, was one detail I shared. We stopped at various places to eat where the drivers obviously had a deal with the owners. One was in the middle of Yugoslavia. The people in the canteen looked at us like we were from another planet. I didn't blame them. We were all drunk or hungover, exhausted from lack of sleep, and wearing strange clothes.

The owners attempted to translate the menu. Joe looked at it and turned to me and said, 'I can understand the burger — but?' He pointed at the laminated poster and next to a picture of some brown stuff they had written 'this'. Aiden took a risk and had it.

'Not bad,' he said. 'Not sure what it is but not bad.'

Back on the bus the no drinking rule wasn't successful. The whole journey turned into a battle of wits with the drivers. It was nerve-wracking, as they seemed to keep one eye on us and one eye on the bendy roads.

The only time they perked up was when Joe told them we were both going to Athens. We had originally decided to go to Thessalonica and then onto Thassos for no other reason than my cousin had been there and said it had nice pine forests. Meeting Aiden and the gang changed our minds. Aiden, a seasoned traveller, had already made arrangements for us to join him.

'Athens?' the driver said. 'No Thessalonica?'

We did a thumbs up and he grinned.

The bonhomie didn't last long though. A couple of hours outside of Athens the driver was so fed up with the carousing and drinking that he stopped and demanded that some people get off.

The mood of people on the bus wasn't that positive towards us. Every time we stopped Joe was the last one back on and he was in constant conflict with the drivers. It wasn't just the drinking. They didn't want him singing, sleeping on the floor, wandering off when we stopped for wee breaks — there was a list of grievances.

We had made a few mates on the bus but most of them just wanted to keep their heads down and get to Athens. But I was fed up. I stood up and shouted, 'You lot don't know how much we've done! It was us who found the coach and your luggage and everything!'

I felt on the verge of hysteria. Joe wanted to get off, but a wave of panic swept over me. I sobbed on his shoulder and begged him not to. I couldn't cope with the thought of hitching after two sleepless nights. Aiden and some others volunteered to get off and hitch a ride and we would take their stuff and join them in Athens.

'It would be easier to get lifts with a chick,' Joe said.

I knew he felt bad and also didn't like to miss out on an adventure. As the coach pulled away the whole bus cheered the renegades standing in the dust at the side of the road. They danced around and threw V-signs up at the drivers. Joe sat morosely for the rest of the journey.

We stayed in a hostel in Plaka called The Square Inn that Aiden had told us about.

He caught up with us quickly and said it was easy to hitch a ride.

Joe nudged me.

It was all soon forgotten though. That first meal and beer sitting in the sun on stable ground with new friends felt wonderful. We decided to keep travelling with Aiden and Rodda — a lovely Welsh guy — who had been there before. We wanted to raise some more money. The next day Rodda and Joe went busking and I wandered round looking at the flea markets with two American girls I had met on the bus. It was nice to have a break from the drinking and carousing and be with some women pottering around pretty shops.

The next day we all took the ferry over to Ios, an island which Aiden assured us would be wonderful. Rodda met up with mates once we got there, and Aiden found a little whitewashed shack that we would share. To get there we walked along the top of stone walls and tried to avoid a grumpy goat with sharp horns.

The beach had one café, a forty-five-minute walk on a donkey track from Ios. We all slept, ate, and cooked in one little room and spent our time sunbathing, walking to and from the town, drinking, eating, and hanging out with the other hippies and travellers who lived in shacks in the area. I carried on writing to Tessa.

God the heat Caruthers, the damned heat. Please ask Jacob to wire us some of Joe's dole money to Athens. I've met someone who used to work in the same pub as me and someone else that used to go out with Lucy the junky — small world. I haven't got a mirror so when I saw myself in a café khazi I had a shock. I'm peeling all down one side of my face — I look like I've got the plague! There are also what looks like flying cockroaches here, so scary!

We lived on bean soup and bread. Occasionally I whipped something up on the one-ring burner. Turning flour and water and onions into pancakes for a load of people at an impromptu party was my famous signature dish.

Most of the time Joe was getting drunk and shouting and singing. Although he was the life and soul of the party, and everyone loved him, I felt tired by it. I heard someone call me 'Joe's caretaker' and I resented it.

'The thing is, it doesn't allow me to have a good time as I'm always worried about what he'll do,' I said to Aiden.

The boys' latest prank happened when they went to get haircuts in the town. When Joe passed out in the barber's chair, Aiden told the bloke to take it all off, so he now had a shaved head and looked like a Hare Krishna. With that, his height and loud Essex accent, he became well known around the island.

Two nights before we went into town, Joe decided that he didn't want to walk back home. He tried to persuade Aiden to help him hotwire one of the few trucks in the island but luckily they couldn't so we walked down the hill and then Joe wanted to cut across the fields instead of walking on the walls. Aiden and I clutched each other in fear and mock whimpering,

'Don't leave me, don't leave me,' we said, as he strode out in the dark into a herd of sheep.

The next day we went for a 'quiet' drink in the local café, just me and Joe as Aiden wanted to apologise to our neighbour whom he had a drunken go at.

I felt like Aiden wanted some kind of hippy threesome with us. I didn't feel attracted to him and treated him like an annoying brother. In the café, Joe met some new people and wanted to spend the evening with them. I was so pissed off that I walked home on my own, braving the goat that I was petrified of (no one told me until the end of our stay that he was actually hobbled and wasn't able to run).

The next day, Aiden and I went in search of Joe as he hadn't come home. I was worried that I'd find him in some girl's bed, but the scene I came upon was not what I had envisioned.

Lying in a sweaty single bed in a room at the back of the tavern, with a dirty blood-stained towel wrapped round his head, I exclaimed, 'What have you done?'

'I'm OK,' he mumbled.

'Like fuck you are,' Aiden said and crouched down to inspect Joe.

'He's got blood coming out of his ear. That's not good.'

He felt his head.

'He feels hot as well.'

Aiden sat back on his heels and said, 'You need to get him to a doc.'

Joe protested and tried to sit up.

'I just need to rest. I'm fine man. I don't need a doctor.'

But Aiden was adamant.

The owner of the tavern was keen to get Joe off his premises. So he helped us load him into his speedboat and we whizzed around the island to the town. I was too scared to be seasick. We propped Joe against a wall while the tavern owner found us the one doctor on the island.

'This isn't good,' the doctor said.

'Blood from the ear is not good. It could be cerebral hemorrhage. You have to take him to Athens.'

Joe started spluttering again, and my heart sank. We had to pay the doctor and take a trip to Athens. This hit our small budget hard. I was also worried about Joe, and about doing all of this on my own.

'You go on next ferry. I cannot take responsibility for him on this island,' the doctor said and banged his hand on the table.

There was nothing for it. I left Joe with Aiden in the waiting room and ran to the ticket office where I got a regular ticket for me and a shared cabin for Joe.

We moved Joe again, his lanky frame almost dwarfing Aiden as he staggered along. We propped him in a café with a glass of water and some sympathetic British tourists. Aiden and I went back to our shack where I stuffed our gear into our holdalls and raced back up the hill to the town. I was covered in sweat, my heart pounding, as we got onto the ferry.

Everyone was kind but there was a feeling from the locals that they wanted us off the island. Dead UK tourists wouldn't do much for their profile and their panic was catching.

The journey took ten hours. As luck would have it, one of our beach gang, George, a handsome Greek man I liked, was on the same ferry. I hoped that he would help us when we got to Athens.

I got Joe settled into his top bunk.

'I don't need to go anywhere, I'm fine,' he said.

'Oh, be quiet, Joe and rest,' I said and felt someone touching my legs. I looked down to see Mr Bottom Bunk having a feel and grinning up at me, patting the bunk next to him. I stalked back out on deck with George and hoped that Joe would be OK.

'Do you want a bite to eat?' George said laying out a full dinner on a bench outside.

I was so relieved that someone was looking after me that I felt like sobbing. George was attractive and great company with his slightly old-fashioned formal English, so the long journey passed quickly. I checked on Joe once but didn't want to be groped again.

As we were docking, I got my things together. It was early evening. George looked at me and said, 'Where will you stay?'

My mouth fell open. I had felt a false sense of security and was counting on George to organize everything and take this scary responsibility away from me.

'I don't know. I guess where we stayed before in Plaka. I don't know anywhere else.'

George nodded. Wearing bright rainbow braces over his jeans and with his curly hair, he looked a little like David Essex in Godspell, with a tache.

He fished around in his jeans for a scrap of paper and a pencil.

'This is the name of the hospital, and this is my number. I'm at work tomorrow but let me know how it goes.'

There was a definite air of wiping his hands of me, so I raised my chin and smiled bravely at him. He waited by our bags while I got Joe and then helped us into a taxi.

At the hostel that night, I didn't get much sleep as I kept waking and checking on Joe. I wrote to Tessa again and told her the ending of the sorry tale.

Please tell Jacob to send money — we're broke! Please, please, please wire it to Post Restante in Athens. And tell my mum what's happened to Joe.

The next morning Joe was still in a stupor but hadn't got any worse and the bleeding had stopped. We got a taxi to the hospital and managed to communicate with a lot of handwaving and broken English. While I did that Joe leaned against a wall sat on a metal chair like some kind of broken-down Lawrence of Arabia with his bloodstained shirt wrapped round his bald head.

We had to buy a ticket for each part of the process and then wait. We got a ticket to see a doctor, then a ticket for an x-ray and then a ticket to see the doctor again for the results. The hospital smelt like hospitals smell everywhere. Everything was clean and busy with crowds of people waiting.

I watched whole families who knew the score pile in with food and company for the sick person. It was lonely just sitting there with Joe who was fairly insensible and not very good company. Then the doctor arrived with the verdict.

'There is no cerebral hemorrhage,' he said, sitting across a highly polished wooden desk with heavy black glasses.

'He has alcohol poisoning and a cut in his ear from where he fell.'

'Where he fell?' I said.

'I kept trying to tell you,' Joe mumbled. 'I fell down.'

With equal amounts of relief and fury, I got Joe out of there and back to the hostel. I bought pita and hummus and ate it on the bed in the dorm we shared. I was ravenous but Joe picked at his and drank some water. I wouldn't let him have beer.

'What shall we do then? We haven't got much money,' I said.

Joe ate a bit of lettuce.

'Dunno really, shall we go back? We've paid for the shack.'

I did a little calculating. We had enough to get ordinary ferry tickets back to Ios and might as well go there as we didn't have enough money to pay for accommodation anywhere else. Even this cheap dorm was setting us back.

'OK then,' I said, settling into my bed. 'We'll go back tomorrow.'

'I told you I was OK. We haven't got a lot of bread left, have we?' Joe said.

I shook my head. We would have to be very frugal, maybe try and get some money sent from home.

When we got back to Ios we were treated like conquering heroes. Everyone wanted to hear our story and stand us drinks and food. The doctor saw us in one of the bars and came over. He looked a bit shamefaced when Joe told him what had happened but insisted it was 'better to be safe than sorry'.

'Ha. I told him,' Joe said after the doctor walked away.

That was his mantra for a while. He recovered quickly and the only thing that curtailed his drinking was lack of money. We drank jugs of local retsina as the cheapest option. It came in red and white and one glorious day it was rose. We asked for that again but it never arrived. Joe did a good pantomime show of getting the red and then the white and mixing them together and the owners of the taverna were very pleased to watch and nod enthusiastically, but then shrugged their shoulders when asked to produce it.

The days slipped by. Over two months passed, and it started to feel like the end of something as summer was almost over. Aiden was getting ready to go to Crete and wanted us to go with him and maybe get some work. Crete seemed to be a jumping off point for lots of people who then continued onto India and beyond. Neither of us were sure. I was a little homesick. We were both worried about money. In the end we had a farewell party and all went our separate ways.

Back in Athens, I sold my watch to get some extra money and Joe sold his camera. Between us we rustled up enough for a bus ticket to Amsterdam where we hoped to meet up with my cousin who lived there and worked for Magic Bus. We also hoped Tessa would send some money. We got the Magic Bus again and made some friends on the coach. We knew the form this time and perhaps weren't quite as overly excited as we had been on the outward leg.

When we got to Rotterdam the driver pulled in and made an announcement: 'We don't go to Amsterdam, too much traffic. We give you money to get the train there and we go on to London.'

Joe and I looked at each other. It would be so easy just to stay on the coach and go to London. We had a quick conflab and decided to continue our adventure.

The driver unloaded our luggage. I was the only woman. The four boys decided to leave me in charge of the luggage while they walked to the train station to see if the money would cover the fares. The driver nodded enthusiastically to all their plans. Once the guys had gone out of sight, he turned to me and said, 'We go now. We waste too much time here, miss ferry.'

'No,' I shouted. 'What should I do?'

'You get back on with us and go to London or stay here.'

I couldn't leave everyone or their luggage, so I just stood there, arms hanging at my side as the coach drove off. I saw the horrified faces of friends we had made on the coach pressed against the windows making 'goodbye' faces.

'Alright for them,' I thought.

When the guys came back there wasn't enough money for the fares and I had left Joe's sleeping bag on the coach.

'Fucking bastards,' Joe spat.

We divvied up what we had. The others headed off and Joe and I went into town so that he could busk. That's why we hadn't sold his guitar that he had lugged all this way. I went to the train station to tell my tale of woe at the ticket office. The guy there was sympathetic but there was no hope for any discount. I paid for our tickets with the coach money topped up with my watch money and what Joe made from singing 'Hotel California' over and over again.

In Amsterdam we couldn't find my cousin at his work. He wasn't there that day, so we stayed the night in a hostel. It looked OK and had crisp white sheets. I was pleased to sleep in a proper bed after the rickety arrangements in the shack and two nights on the coach. We went out for a drink and chips with mayonnaise — my first time ever for this. I heard a voice call our names.

'Oi oi, you two — fancy meeting you here!'

Bob from South London appeared. He was someone we used to hang around with and in fact had been at Sainsbury Road with his girlfriend for our last Christmas there. We caught him up on the gossip and he lent us some money. He had a thriving drug dealing business and during the course of the evening asked Joe if he fancied joining him and staying there.

His girlfriend Lisa looked at me pleadingly. She was a pretty girl wearing a patterned Laura Ashley cotton dress, a white petticoat and a little shawl. But she didn't have much to say for herself and seemed under Bob's spell. He started talking about when they first met.

'I didn't really want to know much about her as I just wanted to get into her knickers. All that what's your star sign bollocks, that can come later,' he said and laughed.

She looked pained but grinned at him.

'It would be great to have another girl around,' she whispered to me.

That night Joe and I discussed Bob's offer. It was more like Joe tried to change my mind. I was adamant.

'I don't want to be one of those drug dealer girlfriends who sits around waiting while the blokes get stoned. I'm no one's 'old lady',' I said.

Joe shrugged. For once I felt so strongly that I was willing to just go home on my own and try to manage my panic.

The next day I found my cousin, Paul, at the Magic Bus offices.

'It's been too long,' he said as I walked up the stairs. He recognised my voice even though we hadn't seen each other for years. He was delighted to see us and sad to hear about his uncle Monty's death.

We arranged to meet when he finished work that afternoon. He had a room in a house that wasn't too far away and said he would stay with his girlfriend for a couple of nights and let us use it. He also said he would lend us what we needed to get tickets home. After not seeing him for eleven years, I felt embarrassed that I couldn't even take him out for a drink. He didn't mind and seemed amused at his little cousin and the fix she was in.

Joe reluctantly agreed to return to London. After being on a sleepy Greek island, the hustle and noise of Amsterdam was disturbing us both. We booked ferry tickets to leave in two days' time.

We spent the day being tourists and visited one of the notorious cafes where you could have a joint. It freaked me out a bit to see that it was OK to smoke a spliff in public. Bob and Lisa met us there and tried to talk us out of going but we showed them the ferry tickets. We also went to the post office but nothing had been left for us. Later on, Paul took us out for pancakes and then we got a bus to his house.

It was in one of the famous tall narrow buildings with a very small room. In his pad he had built a double bed on posts with space underneath to live in. He showed us the kitchen and bathroom and then spent ages on the guitar with Joe learning 'Hotel California'. He laughed when we told him where we had spent the night.

'You're here one night and you find the dodgiest place in Amsterdam,' he said.

Apparently, the hostel had a dreadful reputation. I was scratching and itching and found patches of red all over me.

'Bed bugs,' Joe said.

I was horrified and felt unclean — the hostel seemed so pristine after roughing it.

With little money left, the next day we found a local shop and bought a couple of loaves of bread. We spent the rest of that day hanging out in Paul's room and eating bread with the different spreads we found in the kitchen. It seemed a waste to use our last day in Amsterdam like this, but we had no money to get buses and enjoy its sights. The next morning, with our Greek tans fading, we packed our bags, made some more sandwiches, left the key, and got the bus to the ferry.

Chapter Fourteen

When we got to London we went to my mother's and discussed what to do.

'We could go back to Peckham?' I said.

Joe shrugged and said, 'Don't fancy that. I'll give Jacob a ring and see how he's getting on. We could go and open up another squat in Sainsbury Road.'

The thought of no hot water or outside toilet again made me shudder. In Greece we had no running water and spent three months crapping in a garden. I had earnt a stint of life's luxuries. The first thing I did when we got home was have a long hot bath at my mother's.

Mum was out with 'a friend', Adam said. I had the feeling he had been left on his own a lot. He was fifteen and losing his father had taken its toll. I felt that he had grown up too fast and looked a little lost. Although he seemed to have some good school buddies who liked to pile round and look at Joe with awe as he rolled a spliff and passed it round.

We went to Gatestone Road where we scored on tic and then Joe hotfooted it off to Peckham to see Jacob and pick up some money. There had been some kind of deal between them and I knew that Joe was owed a bit. It would be great until I could get a job. I stayed at the squat and sat in the kitchen chatting to Mik and his girlfriend, Annie, who lived in the room upstairs next to Franz. She was warm and friendly and exactly my age. We had the same birthday too. That made me feel closer to her. She worked in a library and in a veggie café in Streatham.

Annie was a little younger than Mik and seemed quiet next to him.

'So, what we're going to do is get a stencil of a dope leaf and spray it on the hoarding outside the law courts. It'll be a blast. We'll do graffiti about legalizing dope and that will be the first thing they see when they come out,' Mik said.

A classic older hippy, Mik was full of ideas and plans that often didn't happen from what I could glean. He was on the dole, like everyone, but had a thriving dope dealing business and was looking for a new place for him and Annie to live.

'The kitchen is a bit small to share,' Annie said. She was a good cook and a fervent vegetarian. It was nice to wile away some time chatting to her after being with so many blokes for ages.

'Where are you going to live?' I asked Mik.

'Still round here but it's hard to get a rented place if you're on the dole.'

Joe turned up again and we waited with bated breath to hear the Jacob gossip.

'He got on very well in Peckham. His girl was from round there and knew quite a few of the families on the estate so they were quite the toast of the town,' he said. I could feel a 'but' coming.

'But, things have turned a bit sour. He started dealing and pissed off some of the regular dealers.'

Mik nodded his head and said, 'I think his woman is a bit tired of his behaviour. Reading between the lines he may have upset one of her sisters.'

We all laughed.

'Or he may have got off with one of them. It's hard to get a straight story. Anyway, whatever is happening, he's moving on and we need to find someone with a car and collect our stuff.'

'I've got use of a van. I could do it tomorrow,' Mik said.

'Oh man, that's really kind of you,' Joe said.

We made arrangements. I got the feeling that Mik and Annie wanted another couple to be friends with.

That evening I cooked at Mum's and Joe held court with Adam and his mates. They were at that bum fluff stage of being young men who were sweet. Mum rolled in later and was cagey about where she had been. She was cool about us staying; I think it relieved her mind about Adam.

The next day we rocked off to Peckham in Mik's van, rather than the bus, and he parked as near to the flat as he could. The flat looked a bit chaotic and smelt of wee. I hunted for my stuff. Jacob wasn't there. Annoyingly he had gone already.

'Things must've got a bit hot for him,' Mik said.

Jacob's girlfriend snorted. She didn't seem that friendly and just kept shrugging when I asked about my art deco plaques. They were gone, never to be found. Joe was organizing our bits of furniture. Mik just kept going on about the Clarice Cliff china that he had — no help at all.

I found the bed linen my mum had brought me from the US when she was working there. It had been peed on and left on the floor, but at least I had it.

'Where's the little one?' I said.

'Jacob's taken her to his sister's. But this time she's staying. His sister is pissed off at the way he dumps baby there, disappears, and then comes back when he fancies it and picks her up again,' the girl said. Then she cracked a smile, the first one I'd seen. 'I miss that little sprog.'

'Well, it'll be good for her to be in one place,' I said, throwing stuff into plastic bags. Although Mik had been generous with his van, I knew he only had it for a day. When the guys came back from taking the chest of drawers and bookshelves and a box of books, we loaded up with the plastic bags.

'I think we should leave the mattress. It's pissy,' I said to Joe.

'When are you going? I need to give this flat back to the council,' Joe asked the girl.

'Oh, they're taking it back. Jacob already told them because he couldn't afford the rent.'

'Fuck, that was part of the deal. That's screwed us for any other council tenancy,' Joe said.

We split back to my mum's where we did the whole thing in reverse.

'What an amazing house,' Mik said, quite taken aback. It was a big, detached house with art deco style blocks in the front and a large unkempt garden at the back and front. It had a garage and steep drive as well.

'How many bedrooms?' he said.

'Four. But one's a box room. And it's rented,' I said.

'Still really cool.'

I didn't want him to think we were loaded. The truth was we weren't. My childhood had been patchy financially. Sometimes we had foreign holidays and sometimes I was sent to the door to tell the debt collectors no one was in.

My mum was home and Mik was on good form, very charming and funny so she took to him and made tea.

'I'm making a curry this eve,' she said when we had finished and Mik had gone. 'To celebrate.' She was tightlipped until we were all sitting round with a glass of wine, Adam included.

'I'm getting married,' she announced. There was silence.

'Second marriage!' I said.

She gave me a look and I shut up. I had forgotten that Adam didn't know that she was never actually married to Monty. She was too worried about having the same custody battle over Adam that she'd had with my dad over me.

'He won't agree to us living together. He wants to make an honest woman of me.'

She had been going out with him while we were away and getting her feet under the table with his household. She couldn't be without a man to look after her and loved having a load of people to fuss over and boss around. His children were younger than me, self-sufficient teenagers. She was also fed up with market work. I understood that. She had worked hard all her life. It was early starts and very physical carting stuff about in all weather.

'You'll have to meet him,' she said.

And so I did. He seemed nice, a bit lumbering and slow but obviously in thrall to Mum and devoted to her. His eyes followed her around. His three children looked at me suspiciously but were friendly enough. They had an eccentric live-in housekeeper. The house was big and just off South Norwood Hill, not too far. The wedding was scheduled for a couple of weeks.

Joe and I were worried about being on the move again.

'Mum, what are you going to do about the house?' I asked, drying up in the kitchen while she washed the dishes.

'I wondered if you and Joe would like to keep it on?' she said.

I was speechless. I hadn't thought of that. She explained that the rent was protected and very low; we could manage that. We could pay it into her bank account and then she would pay it as normal. I was thrilled and called Joe in.

'We could get someone else in, make it even cheaper,' Joe said.

Mum looked doubtful but she couldn't back down now. Joe and I looked at each other.

'Mik and Annie,' we said together. She had met Mik, so I think she felt satisfied by that.

We went up to Gatestone the next day to tell them and they were delighted.

'It's going to be so cool living with you guys. Such a gas,' Mik said.

We decided that Joe and I would have the living and dining room as our bedroom and living space. Mik and Annie would have mum's bedroom as their living room and my old bedroom as theirs. That left the middle thin bedroom (Adam's room) and the box room as spare rooms. There was a bathroom and separate loo upstairs and another toilet downstairs by the front door. We would have a shared kitchen and shared outhouses.

'Will it be weird? Living in your childhood home with all those memories?' Joe said.

'We'll make new ones,' I said, gripping his arm.

Mum's wedding day came, and I helped her get ready. We were feverishly focused on getting her and Adam to their new home so we could set up our new one. She sat on the bed while I got her dress out.

'I haven't got any tights,' she said and started to cry, looking at me helplessly. 'Am I doing the right thing?'

'Of course you are,' I said, with conviction. Although I had no idea if this was a good move for her. I thought it was as good as any, and I didn't know what else she could do. Selfishly, it was a good move for me.

'I've got a job,' I said, aiming for distraction.

She instantly perked up.

'What? Where?'

'Oh, it's a bit rubbish but brings in some money. I'm doing the Christmas post.'

'Oh, that's great, darling. Money for Christmas.'

She blinked away the tears; ever the optimist my mother and easily diverted.

The wedding felt surreal; all of us looking at each other in the registry office wondering what we were getting ourselves into. Mum and her new husband seemed happy though. They had a reception of sorts in The Conquering Hero, a pub near Crown Point not far from the house.

Mum sent a removal van round for her stuff but took no other part in the process. Joe, Mik and Annie and I stuffed everything we could find in it. We even went under the stairs, the little space that stretched back where I had a den as a child, and took stuff from there. It all went: sofas, wooden coffee tables, brass drinks trolly, huge radiogram, TV, clothes, toys, bunk beds — the lot.

Mum's voice echoed in a cry down the phone line.

'I didn't mean you to send it all over here.'

'What did you think? That we'd be caretakers of all your stuff and just live here surrounded by it?'

'Well, I thought you'd keep the bigger bits at least. We're a bit squashed.'

'Oh, it's a massive house,' I said and left her to it.

She settled in quite happily and tried to mother the two girls. The teenage boy was too old for this, but Adam got on well with him. She got two little Yorkshire Terriers, annoying yappy buggers. Her husband was hesitant and awkward with me, but I didn't mind. As long as he was kind to my mother and looked after my brother my shoulders felt lighter.

Mik and Annie moved in and our arrangement worked well. We weren't far from our friends and the novelty of living in respectable suburbia tickled everyone. The rent was low and easily managed from my postie wages, Joe and Mik's dole, Annie's wages from her now full-time job at the café, and Mik's drug dealing empire.

The first day on the Christmas post, I got up at the crack of dawn, dressed warmly and sensibly, and walked to the sorting office in the dark to get my orders. We were a motley assortment of students and doleys, all looking sleepy with heavy eyes, bewildered at being there. There was a lot of hair sticking up at odd angles and strange clothes.

'Right, you lot,' barked the bright-eyed supervisor.

I felt like someone starting National Service in a Carry On film. Gradually the crowd was allocated jobs until it was just me and a pretty girl in a skirt and platform heels.

'Huh,' I thought, inwardly snorting at her impractical choice of outfit. My face fell though when the male supervisor looked at her indulgently and said:

'Well, you can't do a postman's round my dear in that.'

He put her on the vans where she would sit in the passenger seat, be driven around, and jump out to give parcels.

I got a council estate with loads of flats. My heart sank. I had a phobia of lifts and knew that I'd have to walk up and down a lot of stairs.

'Nice capable girl,' I got told. 'You'll do fine — go with him.'

'Him' was the regular postie who looked harassed at having to show me the ropes. I had a large hessian sack that smelt of oil and must, and I had to lug it around. He would pack everything up for me and the bundles would be in order, so I just had to deliver them. He gave me a map with my 'walk' on it. I had to do this twice a day. Once at 6am and once at 9am and then I was free. I got very fit doing the Christmas posts and loved coming home for breakfast when the boys were just getting up. I've always been an early bird and this made use of it.

I was only in the sorting office four times a day to pick up my bag and hand it in. As Christmas approached, there were decorations up and I could hear laughter and see the odd tin of chocolates and bottle of sherry knocking around. I thought that it looked cosy and fun and wished I'd been put on sorting mail instead of delivering it. I bumped into one of the students I started with and told him this.

'It's a bit lonely out here, bet you have a laugh in there. Wish I could be inside.'

'No, you don't,' he snapped. 'They're fuckers. Took the piss out of me all the time, called me Picasso because I study art. One bloke twisted my nipples with a pair of stapler removers.'

To celebrate Christmas at home we decided to have a massive medieval banquet. I looked up some recipes in a library book and we went all out for it. We took the carpet up in our living room, borrowed some wallpaper paste tables, covered them with sheets and even put hay on the floor (finding it weeks later).

We all pitched in to cook and made some amazing things.

'No lark's heads please, Annie,' Joe teased. She shuddered.

Annie was a skilled cook and I learnt a lot of vegetarian dishes from her. Lentil lasagna and pies made a change from

143

endless spag bol. We spent a lot of time on our outfits. I was a nun with a wimple and veil and some guests rented elaborate costumes. Andy from Camden Hill Road turned up with a wife. A lovely South African woman. They both wore full Tudor jewelled and velvet regalia.

We stretched to a firework display in the garden as well as the meal and it was an evening that people talked about for a long time afterwards. So worth the effort and expense.

After Christmas I got a job at the Queens Hotel, a fairly upmarket hotel not far from us. I went there to see if they had bar work but all they had was a chambermaid post, so I took that. It was boring, back breaking work that paid badly. The only perks were half-used bottles of shampoo left behind by visiting athletes using the sports centre. I once found and kept a pair of knickers belonging to some famous javelin thrower.

One of the women threw her heart and soul into it and soon got promoted to supervisor. We got on well. She would come and sit in rooms with me having a fag and watching TV and then would help me clean.

There was a porter with Indian and Italian heritage who lived in Italy but was here to work and learn English. He had an eye for me, but I told him I had a boyfriend. So he found one of the other chambermaids, a nice Scottish girl, to pair up with and Joe and me used to hang out with them. I met his stylish Italian mother and aunt when they were over on a visit. My shoe had just snapped, and I was walking barefoot. They were horrified but trying to hide it. I was mortified.

I managed to get Joe a job at the hotel as a porter but he lasted one day as he turned up in plimsolls and told them he had no other shoes. They did look a bit strange under his green bellboy outfit and I had to laugh when I saw him.

'I've never seen anything like that in my life!' the manager said, outraged. I considered walking out in sympathy but we needed the money and they needed the staff so they offered me some bar work on top of the chambermaiding to pacify me.

This meant that I would work my day shift as a cleaner then move onto the residents' bar, sometimes work a function bar and then back on the residents' bar until they got fed up and went to bed. The tips were excellent. Especially if there was a function.

'There you are, good girl,' the father of the bride said, giving me a tenner and groping my bum.

I used to prop myself up blearily and accept 'one for yourself' from residents whose toilets I had been cleaning without any tips. During the time I was there only one person left me a tip as a cleaner after I worked hard getting rid of the mess they had made, but they showered me with drinks just for opening a bottle.

Chapter Fifteen

We were enjoying our life in the suburbs and getting on well with Mik and Annie. We redecorated the downstairs living room in white with green wallpaper in the alcoves. The dining room became our bedroom with an arch separating the rooms. From the ceiling, we hung a huge silk parachute. At night with twinkly lights and cushions it looked like a Bedouin tent. In the day you could see the outline of the room behind it.

Mum came round one day and said she was upset to see the house and 'what you've done to it.' I thought it was an improvement. In particular, she was upset about the upstairs bedroom which was now Annie and Mik's living room. They had fallen asleep naked in front of an electric fire and the carpet caught a spark. There was a lot of nude yelping and water being thrown. Now the carpet had an unsightly melted patch with a rug over it.

I thought things were going well with Mum's new husband and family. Whenever I spoke to her she seemed optimistic and positive. But one day Adam turned up with a bag.

'I don't like it there,' he said.

I asked him what the matter was.

'He shouts.'

'Where are you going to stay, Ad?' I said.

He shrugged.

'I dunno, here?'

His old room was free, so I called a house meeting and explained the situation.

'I can't say no,' I said to Annie and Mik. Annie looked pained and Mik flicked the ash from his fag into a saucer.

'Well, this whole house is your gig so whatever you want,' he said.

Adam moved into his childhood bedroom and straight away his mates started coming round. They were a lively crowd, still teenagers, and liked to have a party and take drugs. That suited Joe. They looked up to him as the big hippy who had trodden the path before and he enjoyed being an idol, especially to the girls.

By this time I had yet another job, a summer job at the children's zoo in Crystal Palace. Tessa got a job there too.

It was great work but there were early morning starts and it was very physical. So I needed to keep regular hours and get enough sleep, which wasn't happening in our house. I hardly ever saw Joe as he stayed up late. I felt we were unraveling a bit.

Having Adam around was great and I liked most of his mates. The atmosphere was super charged with energy. There was a buzz in the air that made me feel I was on the end of a precipice staring over and unsure what was lurking below in the depths.

I loved the animals and children. The zoo team were friendly and gave me something new to focus on. New interests and different friends that were separate from Joe and not revolving around smoking dope and getting high.

In charge of the zoo was a lesbian who would only employ other women.

'Because men are useless,' she said, a tall, imposing and slightly scary woman. She couldn't bear my fear of a Sarus crane called Percy.

'But when he comes for you, he's at your waist,' I wailed. 'When he comes for me, it's my eyes.'

She tutted with impatience when I accidentally let some monkeys out and cried until a more experienced worker took pity on me and helped me herd them back in. I thought she didn't like me, but I was told by a worker:

'If she doesn't like you, she doesn't speak to you — you're OK.'

Tessa and I learnt loads of animal skills and the atmosphere was like a crowd of jolly girl guides. Occasionally, we had staff outings and went to a disco in Croydon called Rockefellas.

'This one is for the zoo girls,' the DJ would say and we'd roar and stamp about on the dance floor.

I was the fittest I had ever been from hauling animals and bales of hay around. When I went home in my zoo uniform, I got a few admiring glances from my brother's mates much to my brother's chagrin. As part of my job, we travelled round the more deprived areas of London with a horse box and a selection of animals to show children who had never seen anything like them.

Sometimes I was frightened and exhausted. Often I was elated. For the first time it felt like useful and interesting work rather than just a way to make money.

Joe and I drifted further apart. He started working in an adventure playground in Lambeth and we decided to have our own personal money for the first time.

We did come together to perform in a street theatre group for children called 'Show Off Shows'. A friend wrote a great slapstick sketch involving a mother and father in a café with a

148

policeman. It had some political undertones and some effective props including pretend 'sick' that made the children in the audience scream in horror. We got some funding from Lambeth and performed at a festival in Kew Gardens and at the launch of the refurbished Lambeth Walk.

It was raining that day and only a few gathered to watch us. They got impatient and liberated the bowl of sick and started to throw it around.

'Quick, run! It's getting out of hand!' Joe shouted.

We sheltered ourselves from the audience in the Citizen's Advice Centre.

Our last performance was down in the squats where we used to live off Gypsy Hill.

'Teenagers Alley,' Joe called it. 'We were the first,' he sniffed.

The empty houses were now occupied. A thriving scene had emerged with three squatted streets. The Peanut Factory was operating as a community centre. Joe and I performed at a street party in the area. We were both working full-time and didn't have the energy to expand the theatre group, so that was our swan song.

* * *

'We're moving out,' Mik said.

He looked anxious as he told us. He was always thin, but that day looked gaunt in his skintight patched jeans and tie-dyed shirt. He had kept true to the hippy dress code. Punk had passed him by although I suspected he dyed his blond curls. I hadn't seen much of Annie recently and there had been raised voices, unusual for them.

'Where are you going?' Joe said.

'Annie is getting her own place and I'm moving back into my room in Gatestone. I don't really want to live with a teenager; no offence to Adam, but we had a good scene going here.'

I could see his point. The place certainly had a different vibe now. It was younger but could be challenging with the noise and level of drug taking. They both left. Adam had a separate room to hang out in and we had our living room back.

Shorty after that my mum called in tears and said, 'I can't live with him anymore.' She said her relationship with her husband had broken down. He was depressed and moody and she found his children difficult. They were used to doing their own thing and didn't take kindly to her trying to mother them.

'Can I move back?' she pleaded. 'I just want somewhere to lay my head while I sort myself out.'

The little fourth bedroom was empty and she said it would be fine.

'You won't notice that I'm here. I'll be quiet and you just carry on,' she said.

That didn't last long.

We continually snapped at each other. She kept talking about how this had been her house, and how she couldn't bear how it looked now and everything was so awful. There were daily dramas. It didn't help my relationship with Joe.

'We've got to do something,' I hissed at him one evening as we lay in our downstairs bedroom with a constant ear out for my mother's footsteps. She had nowhere else to go apart from 'our' living room.

'I'll go to Gatestone Road and ask them,' he said.

'They haven't got any room there.'

'They've got the whole floor at the top.'

'That's true. It would be better for the house if it was being heated and lived in.'

We went the next day. Franz, Mik, and Johnny were all happy with the idea. Mik had no quarrel with us.

'I thought this would happen,' he said shaking his head at my tales of Mum's drama.

We went upstairs to the top floor. The back room was too decrepit to use; the windows were smashed, and it was full of junk. There were remnants of a wasp's nest on top of the broken furniture. The front room would do as a small living room. Next to it was a smaller space just big enough for a double mattress and a chest of drawers. In between the back room and the living room was a strange long room that I had plans to use as a walk-in wardrobe. The other side of the back room was the padded cell.

This was the room they had used as a primal scream room, but they slacked off with this now and agreed that we could use it as a kitchen. It must have originally been one as it did have a tap in it. Now it was a strange and eerie place with layers of egg boxes and felt covering the walls, ceiling, window, and floor. Everything was muffled in there. I did an exploratory scream and Joe couldn't hear it outside.

'I feel like staying in there a while and having a good go,' I said. Joe looked at me and rubbed my shoulder.

'I'll leave you to it.'

I stayed in there and had a few shouts and groans. The situation with my mother had frayed my nerves and I could feel the old panic and anxiety returning. I got bored with shouting and thought I'd make a start on getting the felt covering off. I pulled a section off and it made my flesh creep; it looked like some kind of fungus or animal. Suddenly a packet fell down. I picked it up and examined it. It was a wodge of cash. I counted it, £400. Very nice.

Trying to suppress my excitement I called Joe.

'What?' he kept saying, but eventually I heard his footsteps dragging up the wooden stairs. He had a joint in his hand.

'Look!' I said and his irritation vanished.

'Fuck me, that's a lot of bread.'

'Yes, but whose is it?' I said.

We both sat down on the floor and looked at it. Joe counted it again. I wondered if he was thinking the same as me.

'That would help do this place up,' I said, fanning it out in my hands. 'And it would be going into the house.'

He rocked back on his heels, frowning.

'I don't think we could do it, babe,' he said. 'It would be bad karma. It belongs to someone.'

'Yes, but who? They obviously haven't missed it. It's been here ever since they did the room. Perhaps it's someone who has moved away.'

'You hope that's the case, but you know it's not,' Joe said and started humming. Then he came to some kind of decision, stood up, dusted the dirt off his jeans, and shoved the wedge into his back pocket. I felt aggrieved. It was me that had found it and now he was making all the decisions.

'There's only one thing we can do. We just ask if anyone has lost anything. They're all here at the moment, so let's get it over,' he said and held out a hand to help me to get up. I was grumpy.

'Well at least let me ask. And don't give any details, keep shtum,' I said, hoping that no one would say they'd lost anything and we could keep it and make a few of the squalid rooms into a habitable living area.

We called Johnny up from his basement lair and sat in the living room on a mattress.

'Oooh, house meeting. Haven't had one of those for a while. That's a new energy,' Mik said.

'I was ripping the felt off the walls and came across something,' I said and felt like a character in an Agatha Christie book. 'We wondered if any of you had lost anything.'

Franz and Johnny both shook their heads, but Mik looked interested.

'What kind of thing?' he said, jittery and tapping his hand against his leg, his skinny frame shaking.

Joe and I looked at each other.

'Have you lost anything?' I said, unwilling to give up my interrogation so quickly.

'Well, I might have. It's hard to remember when we were doing that room.'

'It's money,' Joe said, and I could have hit him. Mik's face lit up.

'Yes, that's right, I remember now. I stashed some bread in there for safe keeping in case the pigs came round for alimony.'

I thought the cash probably was his but felt aggrieved at the loss of it and at Joe for being a blab.

I held out my hand to Joe and said, 'Give it here then. I found it.' As I placed the dough in Mik's hand I asked if I would get a finder's fee. No such luck.

'Oh man, I really need that bread at the moment and it's amazing that you found it. It's a good omen for you moving in. I'll nip out and get chips for everyone and some beers,' he said.

'Well, that's something,' Joe said to me later when we were tucking in. I held my hand out for the vinegar bottle, not ready to forgive him yet.

'Yes, well we could've had a cut of it,' I said, loud enough for Mik to hear but he chose to ignore it. I also wondered if there was more up there.

'At least he'll help rip the rest of that crap down,' I said to Joe when we were walking home. I was still working and Joe spent every spare moment at Gatestone getting the place ready. At least I hoped he was doing that and not just sitting in the kitchen smoking dope with Franz and Mik.

We were ships in the night and Adam's crowd missed their guru, but Joe was making progress. We bought a secondhand electric cooker and fridge and he cobbled together a sink and unit. There was one cold tap and a couple of old cupboards we found on skips. It was a standard squat kitchen and good enough. I was desperate to get out of my mum's house.

Things came to a head with Joe one morning to throw a spanner in the works. It was my birthday. I had the weekend off and we were planning to go to a park and then out to my old pub The Queen's Arms in the evening. Joe had disappeared upstairs the night before for a session with the young gang, and I had gone to bed alone. In the morning the house was quiet, and I woke up stretched like a starfish in the double bed. I crept upstairs to use the bathroom and see where Joe was.

Adam's 'living room' door was open and Joe was there with one of Adam's friends, Hayley, in bed. They were having sex. I was horrified and shocked and didn't know what to do. I let out a muffled cry that they must have heard, but I felt too shaky to confront them fully. I went downstairs crying and feeling like the world had come to an end. Joe (not very quickly) followed me. I heard a scuffle at the front door, then he came into the bedroom and put his arms round me.

'Look, we can sort this out now and have a row or we can have a nice time on your birthday and talk about it later. She's gone anyway.'

I sniffed, choking back tears.

'OK,' I managed to say. Then I pushed him away and slowly got washed and dressed.

Adam saw me, and couldn't meet my eyes but muttered, 'Happy birthday, sis.' I think he was up long enough the night before to see what was happening. I didn't blame him as he was just a kid.

Joe's friend from Kew had stayed overnight in the living room and we all went out to Blackheath Park as planned. He must have noticed the strained silence and lack of birthday fun as he left after a subdued lunch in the café. In the evening we went to the pub and met a whole crowd of people.

I got drunk. It seemed the right thing to do and a big crowd of us piled back to Gatestone Road after the pub. There was something in the air that evening — a sense of danger, possibilities, recklessness, and excitement. The young crowd were with us, and I was teasing one of them about his lovely cheekbones. He looked a little like David Bowie. Me, Tessa, and Annie had all admitted a slight interest in him. That evening the brakes were off and I felt slightly insane.

The normal rules and structures melted away. Joe disappeared upstairs and people started leaving. Cheekbones and I were the only ones sitting by the fire. We passed a bottle of wine back and forth. He turned to me.

'Would you give me a birthday kiss?' he said. I had no hesitation, and we spent the night together on a mattress in the living room. At one point I went upstairs to get a cigarette and I found Joe in bed with Pam. I felt numb and didn't care anymore. She had always liked Joe and often told me I was lucky to be with him. I realised she was just waiting for her chance and wondered if our friendship meant anything to her.

'Good luck to her,' I muttered to myself.

The next day Joe and I went home separately. I went to work in a state of shock. In a childish way I felt the tables had turned and the score was even. I think Joe felt it too but in a different way. That evening he explained.

'I felt relieved about what happened last night,' he said. 'It means we can go forward having an open relationship which is what I've always wanted.'

I looked at him in disbelief. I knew at that precise moment our relationship was over.

Joe and I had planned a few days away together after my contract at the zoo had finished. We were staying with Joe's friends in the North of England that I hadn't met before. During that time we were polite and friendly to each other and managed to have a good time. I told one of the women that we were breaking up and she was astonished.

'I actually thought that you seemed so well suited and happy together,' she said.

That evening when we came back to my mum's house Joe went off to see Pam and I met up with Tessa. We sat in silence drinking tea.

I bet she's been there all this time he's been 'doing up Gatestone',' I said.

Tessa looked awkward and fiddled with her nails then said, 'I did see her there sometimes when I went round to see Johnny. I didn't think anything of it at the time. You and Joe have been together so long. What are you going to do now?'

Tessa had recently moved into a rented house with Annie. I was fucked if I was going to scuttle off to a little bedsit on my own.

'I'm going to Gatestone,' I said. My nana always told me that when a situation was bad, 'Spit on the floor, wipe your mouth, and move on.' I was going to do that and felt full of resolve.

When I finally saw Joe, I said, 'I'm moving into Gatestone to the top floor as planned.'

He looked astonished.

'If you're doing that, I'll have to move into the room underneath with Pam. I've got nowhere else, and she's left her boyfriend, so she hasn't got anywhere to go,' Joe said.

'That's Mik's room.'

'With that bread we found he's gone off. Gone walkabout. No one knows where.'

'I don't care if you're in that room,' I said. 'It's the least you can do. I'm having the upstairs and you can do what you want.'

I moved in, but there were a few things that still needed doing in the kitchen and I kept asking Joe to do them. I knew Pam was furious. It wasn't at all what she had planned and one day she came upstairs to tell me that.

'Joe isn't your boyfriend anymore, and I'm fed-up seeing people I don't know around the house.'

I shrugged. I had halfheartedly been seeing Cheekbones and he came round with some other friends. We were all a bit noisy.

'Well, you've got Joe and I can have whoever I want,' I spat at her.

That tipped her over the edge.

'I haven't GOT anyone,' she shouted and stormed off.

There was some relief in baiting her. Otherwise seeing them moon about the place being love's young dream could get to me. Johnny caught me sobbing once in the big living room.

'Thoughtless fuckers,' he muttered, awkwardly putting an arm round me. I knew all of our friends thought Pam was out of order and awful. That gave me consolation.

'It's both of them, though,' I said to Annie one night when we met up in the pub.

'Yes, but I heard that Joe wanted to live with both of you. But Pam wouldn't have it.'

I snorted and spluttered on my drink. I needed my friends to cheer me up as I had recently knocked on the new lover's door to ask Joe about fixing something in my kitchen and glimpsed them having sex before I carefully shut the door again.

It was just too much.

Chapter Sixteen

I settled into my new flatlet and relished having my own space. To combat the perishing cold, I bought a Calor gas heater. Someone gave me a portable black and white TV as a present and I spent a lot of time curled round my heater watching the TV, a new experience for me.

I didn't have a record player but had got rid of much of my vinyl anyway, so I had a little cassette player and a few cassettes — Sex Pistols, Iggy Pop, Elvis Costello, The Jam. I painted my rooms cream and brown and the kitchen white and red gloss. I even tackled the stairs — lime green gloss. I did them in sections making sure one bit was dry before I did the next. I tripped with the cat tray and embedded granules in the wet paint.

Big Puss had kittens while we were living at my mum's and I found homes for all of them. One went to Adam who really wanted a kitten. Inevitably he couldn't handle it at his stepfather's and the poor little thing weed and shat everywhere. The whole household hated it. He asked if I would take it back, so I did. Little Puss returned to be hissed at and spat at by her mother. This time I did it better and had her spayed and vaccinated.

Johnny was ingenious. He constructed an amazing cat run for the cats. It went out the toilet window (which meant we had to keep the window open all year round even when it was freezing) to a wooden pathway down the side of the building then to the top of the back gate where little steps led down to the garden.

'Bloody hell, they'll never manage that,' Tessa said.

But they did, and one of their favorite pastimes was defending the slope outside to hiss and bat, ambushing the other cat coming down. It was disconcerting when a cat suddenly appeared at the window and jumped down when you were having a private moment.

The loo had a massive old-fashioned cistern with a heavy pull chain and stained thick wooden seat. It was grim. I had the bright idea of cheering it up by spraying the whole thing silver.

'Fuck me,' Joe said when he saw it, but he laughed and Pam sniffed. It did mean that whenever it got a bit stained, we could just give it another coat.

'David Bowie's bog,' Tessa christened it.

'Bad news,' Joe said one day when I came in from work. He was sitting in the kitchen with Franz.

'Oh no, tell me,' I shouted.

'It's one of the cats,' he said and got up and came towards me. I wanted it to be Little Puss as Big Puss was such a part of my life with Joe.

'It's Big Puss,' he said and wrapped me in his arms as I sobbed against his shoulder. I could feel he was weeping as well. The death of Big Puss was another nail in the coffin of our time together. It was hard to remember his betrayal and keep angry when I remembered the good times we'd had together. I also tried not to be too bitter towards Pam.

Big Puss had ventured out to the road and been run over. We buried her in the back garden. Little Puss seemed to like the undivided attention. She stayed upstairs a lot because there was now a dog in the house.

Franz had found a girlfriend and they were glued together. In a spirit of togetherness, they decided to get a puppy. They called her Wuffel.

Franz looked fondly at the puppy when he told us the name. Then it went into the living room and weed on the floor. Upon hearing the name, Pam turned to me and made sick faces behind Franz and Polly's back as they rushed to clean up. I had a spark of comradeship with her and wondered if we could ever be friends again. I wanted to. I wasn't someone to hold grudges and knew she was just an element in a relationship that was going down the pan anyway.

I made a bead curtain for the bedroom using beads that I bought by the bucketful from a bead shop. It was heavy. I had to use fishing wire to thread it and suspended it from a piece of wood. It made a satisfying clacking noise as I went in and out.

I was working again. I was inspired by Joe's tales of the adventure playground in Lambeth. I reflected on the zoo and realised that I liked the children more than the animals (less biting), so I looked around for something near me.

I found Crystal Palace Adventure Playground. Run by the GLC, I wandered in to see if they needed staff.

It took a while to get past the gate into the playground as a crowd of young people were sitting on it shouting 'No parents' as I tried to get in. Eventually I was directed to a brick-built hut where more teenagers were playing pool. There was a glassed-in office at the front where an imposing man sat behind a desk.

'Well, it's quite busy here. We could do with someone extra,' he said, a big thickset man with a beard looking at me suspiciously. I was taken aback. This wasn't the alternative hippy crowd I had imaged from Joe's descriptions of his workplace.

'Come back tomorrow for a trial day and we'll see how you get on,' the bloke said then got up and shouted out the window: 'Get off your bike.' Some poor little kid nearly fell over in his haste to get off. I wasn't sure about this; the bloke and the crowds of young people worried me. I thought I would be with little children.

The next day I turned up for work and was taken round and shown the ropes (literally we had to put up rope swings). Dave, the bloke, and his wife ran the playground. Their children were around as well. During the day some school groups used the space, but mainly local unemployed boys hung out there. It was hard to tell the staff from the kids as some of them had been coming to the playground and then been employed straight out of school. In this male-dominated atmosphere, I was glad to be with Dave's wife who took me on a tour, showed me the huts, the areas with the rope swings, and the wood at the back. She also told me the extensive list of rules.

'Someone always has to be on the gate, and we don't allow parents in.'

'Why not?' I asked.

She shrugged.

'Dave finds it better that way.'

Children had to be aged five to fifteen but there seemed to be a select few who weren't. I had an overwhelming feeling of being the new kid on the block but at that moment a school party of young children came in and I was put to work — helping them on the outside structures and doing some quiet outdoor painting on a table.

'You'll do,' Dave said at the end of the day. 'Come tomorrow and I'll get him to talk to you.'

I had no idea who 'him' would be. It turned out to be a soft-spoken Welsh man who was Dave's supervisor. He mainly stayed in his GLC office in Burgess Park and looked pained a lot of the time when Dave bellowed at him.

'You said just have her for one day but I'm not getting rid of her,' he shouted at the Welsh man. I was embarrassed as I was being used as a pawn in their power struggle but interested to see what would happen. I also needed the work.

'OK,' the Welsh man said. 'As you say you need someone else, we'll put Deborah (smiles at me) on a temporary contract and see how it goes. Let's say six weeks to start with.'

That was the beginning of my career on the adventure playground.

At Gatestone Road the residents were on the move and there was a lot of shuffling around of rooms. Mik went on the missing list for a while and then came back. He couldn't live at Gatestone as his room had gone but he might as well have as he was round all the time.

Franz split up with his girlfriend, went travelling as a roadie for a rock band, returned quickly bringing back Wuffel, and moved back in. Johnny and I stayed put. In the attic I was domesticated and secure. I put up a little window box by whacking massive nails into the wood of the window frame. Franz wasn't sure about it.

'Looks positively dangerous,' he said.

* * *

'Let's go out,' Tessa said one evening. 'It's so boring round here. There's a new club in Brixton on the main road. It's the opening night — let's go.'

163

We got a few people together and went. New Romantics were in full bloom; I loved this movement as it involved taking a lot of time and effort to get ready. It was in sharp contrast to what was going on in the streets at the time. There was unemployment, social injustice, poverty, riots, filthy streets from bin strikes, yet we could spend a whole day making outfits, spraying our hair, and putting on makeup for a night out. The glamour and decadence went hand in glove with the grime and hard times. When I was younger and living at home, I was a member of the Worker's Revolutionary Party, an extreme left-wing group led by Vanessa Redgrave and her brother Corin. Now my life was my political activism as I lived in a squat, worked with unemployed youth for the GLC, and went out clubbing. Getting dressed up and partying was a living protest against cuts and poverty. It was fingers up to the government.

The club was called The Fridge. It was glittering white, decorated with lots of fake ice stalagmites and stalactites.

I thought it was a perfect venue. No one used the cloakroom. A girl wearing a cute bodysuit and pillbox hat stood behind the counter, hangers at the ready, with a hopeful expression waiting for tips, but we all passed her by. We didn't have the money and didn't want to queue at the end of the evening. Our tatty men's jumble sale tweed coats could be scrunched up and rolled in a corner. We didn't care if beer and fag ash got on them.

I wanted to shed my coat to show off my outfit, a white and gold suit with elbow length gloves. It was nippy in there though and we all huddled on a bench seat.

'I suppose it makes sense — The Fridge,' Tessa said. It did look gorgeous — lit up with silver and blue lights to get a cold icy backdrop. The DJ started playing 'Wham Rap' and we got on the dance floor. We were dancing together, a strange kind of hand turning fast jive that I had seen other people do and was easy to copy. It was soon packed and got warm, condensation running down the blue icy walls and the Fridge became a sauna.

We left in the early hours and shared a cab back. I didn't have long to sleep but I wasn't at work until 11, so I didn't care. Tea and toast after a club was the best thing ever. My social life had consisted of the pub and sitting around in a living room in a cloud of dope smoke.

Now my nightlife started expanding and I was excited at being able to drink and be out after pub hours. I regularly went to the West End clubs as well as The Fridge. With a few of us the taxi home wasn't expensive, and the evening was far more interesting and exciting than a grotty pub or a living room. We smuggled in cheap drink and had one expensive glass from the bar.

People made an effort and dressed up. There was glamour, music, and dancing! I loved to dance, and apart from the Tuesday evenings in Camden Hill Road and the odd party I had no opportunity. There was also the possibility of seeing someone famous. I often saw Boy George and other stars in the Whisky A Go Go (WAG) club.

The best and most perfect club experience was at a club called Le Beat Route (The Beetroot). Tessa's sister, Lou, and I went there for a mod night. We cobbled together our best approximation of a mod look and to our delight the club was filled with real die-hard mods.

The mod movement had been revived recently; possibly because of The Jam, and a younger crowd hunting out tonic suits, Ben Sherman's, Fred Perry's, and feather cuts. I vaguely remembered it from the first time around but loved it now. My main love was the music. I adored the energy and pulse of punk in the early days but felt that it was male dominated and just involved jumping up and down. It was thrilling in contrast to the laid-back hippy era that I had been part of.

'Hippies are dope and punk is speed,' Andy said to me, and he was right.

I spent hours looking at the album cover to Crosby Stills Nash and Young on that porch in that house in Laurel Canyon wondering what life was like in LA. I didn't have to do that with punk. I knew what life was like in late 70s London — I was there! It felt much more immediate and real to me. Now I had moved on and I loved New Romantics and also Motown. The Beetroot mod night played it back-to-back.

'Look, look,' Lou hissed in my ear.

I couldn't believe it — Paul Weller and Bruce Foxton from The Jam walked into the club both in their best stay press suits. It caused a frisson in the club but the clientele were too cool to gawp much. The dance floor got crowded when they hit it. Lou and me shot up and did our best moves. They didn't notice us but The Sunday Times did. They were also there to capture the mod revival for the colour supplement and snapped photos of us.

'I can't believe this is happening!' Lou said.

The drink had made me reckless and when Paul Weller was up at the bar I ambled up 'casually'. We nodded at each other, as you do at a bar, standing and both trying to get the bar staffs' eye. Then I thought, fuck it, and turned to him.

'Can I have your autograph,' I asked, feeling all shades of pathetic.

'Sure,' he said. 'Got a pen?'

'No, I haven't. You're a rock star, you should always have a pen.'

He had the grace to laugh at that, then borrowed one from the bar staff and scribbled his name on a torn bit of cardboard I had found on the floor.

I mumbled thanks and scuttled back to Lou to display my trophy. The whole evening sparkled and we couldn't wait to get back and tell everyone about our brush with the famous. In the cab on the way home I turned to Lou who was half asleep.

'It was probably just a really boring shit night for them though,' I said.

'Whaaaat?'

'The Jam, it was nothing to them but so amazing for us — makes you think, doesn't it?'

'Mmmm,' she agreed, snuggling into my shoulder.

If we weren't 'Up West' at clubs then we were out in pubs watching bands. The alternative cabaret scene was huge in the early 80s with regular nights in big pubs in Brixton and Herne Hill. One night we saw The Thompson Twins and when I went to the loo afterwards Alannah Currie, the lead singer, was trying to get out of her boiler suit.

'You were great,' I said and she smiled, graciously.

She was trying to get away from a very drunk Irish woman who was grabbing her and repeatedly saying: 'You sounded just like Thin Lizzy. Just like them. Completely the same.' Over and over like it was the greatest compliment she could give. From the look on her 'just sucked a sour lemon' face, I don't think she felt complimented.

We also started to follow a band called The Remipeds and knew someone in the brass section. They had a great sound and always started their gig with Hawaii Five-O trumpets and sax.

With such a busy social life it was good that sometimes I didn't have to do much at the adventure playground. Weekends and school holidays were busy but during the week I could just sit and play chess and board games with children and do the odd bit of craft. I grew to realise that age wasn't an indicator of how good anyone was at chess.

'Give you a game?' said an angelic little eight-year-old in the chair opposite me.

'Sure,' I said setting out the pieces. 'Played before?'

'Once or twice.'

Five minutes later I had to resign as I was soundly check mated.

Chapter Seventeen

While I was up at Gatestone 'teenagers alley' down the hill was filling up. Tessa and Lou lived there as did loads of other people I knew. The hum of creativity mainly centered around The Peanut Factory. Most of the houses in the triangle of three roads were squatted and a few had the original residents. They had to be open minded and probably slightly deaf. Most people were on the dole and spent all day going in and out of each other's houses drinking tea, eating toast, and trading gossip.

Love affairs, one-night stands, heartbreak, joy, betrayal — teenagers alley had it all. It was a mix of complete squalor, cold grubby houses with no hot water and outside toilets, and fanciful glamour — feather boas, beaded cocktail bags, vintage suits. The counterculture in all its glory. I left a long-term relationship where I had been faithful although I was beginning to realise that Joe hadn't. I started to have many short-term, not relationships, more like encounters. I was falling in and out of passion, love, and crushes — whatever they were called. I hadn't learnt that being friends with a bloke didn't mean that I had to sleep with them. I could just be a mate. It was a painful lesson.

'No, not him, I can't believe it!' Tessa cried. 'Why?'

'Oh, I don't know. I was a bit drunk, and it was his birthday,' I said, hanging my head and looking at my shoes.

Some of these flings turned into friendships, but the best times were with my gang of girls, getting ready to go out and wondering who we might bring home or go home with. The most fun would be endlessly discussing who our latest crush was and how we could corner them. I think many men were dismayed by how strong and riotous we were as a group. It felt a bit like singling out and hunting down prey. The payoff was the discussion afterwards rather than the connection and the sex.

That was what it was like for me anyway. I was still close to Tessa but also to one of Adam's mates, Melanie. Lou was young but managed to get into pubs and clubs.

'It's my eighteenth birthday. Can we have a party at Gatestone?' she said.

The downstairs rooms were made for parties — two massive Edwardian reception rooms linked by heavy folding wooden doors. We arranged for one of the bands from the Gypsy Hill squats to play, King Kurt, a loud rockabilly band known for throwing food about at their gigs. The last time I had seen them there were all sorts of chicken offal being hurled about. That I didn't fancy, but Lou's party was a great success and offal-less.

There was a big rockabilly scene down at the squats, with King Kurt and other fledgling bands, and a lot of quiffs and hair gel. Parties happened every weekend. It was amazing how many people could cram into a small Victorian terrace.

'How are you doing, Barry?' I said to a skinny older-looking bloke with a hangdog expression. He'd come round to score.

'Oh, you know man. OK, I guess, it's so fucking cold here though,' he said, pulling his old black jacket closer round him and wiping fag ash off his skinny black jeans. He crossed his legs and his scuffed black boot jiggled like a smack addict needing a fix. LA Barry, as we called him, wasn't a junkie though. He smiled wolfishly, his greasy dark hair hanging in threads down the sides of his lean face.

'You know, I just can't seem to get it together here.'

I wasn't sure what 'it' was or what it would look like. I couldn't really imagine LA Barry actually doing anything. He looked over the top of my head and blew out a stream of smoke.

'You know, I can't wait—'

Lou and I looked at each other delightedly. Here it was, the line we had all been waiting for. The one that gave him his name.

'Yeah, I can't wait to be back in LA. When I'm there, man I can really get it together, you know?' We all nodded, pretending we knew what he was going on about. He took another drag and said, 'Yeah, that's where I can really get things going, you know? I'm just existing here, but in LA things will be different. It'll all happen when I get back to LA.'

He wasn't American or anything, so we couldn't quite work it out. Years later Tessa went to LA to catch up with Johnny. She also bumped into LA Barry who had finally saved up the money and challenged his inertia and made the move.

'And you know what,' she said. 'He was exactly the same. Skinny and in black in all that sun AND he was talking about Gypsy Hill as the place where he really got it together.'

171

The squats were full of people like that, characters who seemed to just be parachuted there. I had no idea who they really were, where they had been, and why they were there. One or two had a permanent furtive air and a way of looking over their shoulders that made me think they were on the run. There was a fair sprinkling of actual runaways as well, young rascals who had fled home. Mixed in the cocktail were earnest politicos, members of the SWP who had the houses with constant meetings and crowds of dilettante would-be artists wafting around in kimonos.

It was a heady mix to dip in and out of.

* * *

I was finally earning a steady wage at the playground as Senior Playleader. I had paid holiday leave and sick pay. In Gatestone Road we paid council tax, electricity, and water bills but no rent. The house was owned by a housing society and the agreement was that we would pay the utilities and move out when they wanted the house back. Owners had to pay double tax on unoccupied properties, so this was a good deal for them. They also knew that the house would be kept warm and in repair, well better than if it was derelict anyway.

As a result, although I didn't live with many amenities, I did have spare cash sloshing around for the first time in my life. So, I decided to have driving lessons and buy a car — a 1962 powder blue Morris Minor that we used to drive to a party in Camden. Me and Tessa very big-eyed at this part of North London. I loved the car but wasn't a confident driver, so other people drove me around.

I knew Earls Court and Kensington where my nana lived. As a teenager, in the 70s, I loved getting on the 49 bus and going down the Kings Road and Kensington High Street. I spent a lot of time in Biba, both the smaller one and the huge department store and shops like Granny Takes a Trip. An exciting outing for my friends and me was trawling round the hippy stalls in Kensington Market. More recently we discovered Let it Rock which became Sex, Vivienne Westwood's shop, and loads of secondhand clothes shops in Worlds End. I also liked Covent Garden, another special outing, often a birthday treat with cocktails at Café Paradiso. A friend who worked there told us that Kid Creole and the Coconuts came there when they were in town so we always had hope this might happen again.

Apart from being in the West End for shopping and clubs and Kensington I didn't know London at all.

'It's really a collection of villages,' I said to Tessa as we pressed our noses at the window on the way to the party looking at the unfamiliar terrain. 'I only really know the Palace, Streatham, Brixton, and Norwood.'

'And Croydon,' Tessa reminded me. We had both worked in shops in Croydon and as a teen I had hung out in St George's Walk with all the hippies there. I gave a fake shudder, happy those days were behind me.

The party and being in a new place with people we didn't know was novel. We felt like real explorers. I don't actually remember all that much about it except that I started talking to a German guy who lived in Berlin and played the saxophone.

'Just your type,' Tessa said, counting off on her fingers. 'Plays sax like your dad, mad eyes and big nose — perfect.'

She did have a point. I gave him my phone number (we had a phone in the hall at Gatestone) and he phoned me during the week. Although it was a stilted conversation, we arranged to meet in an alternative comedy night that week in Brixton. There was no way I was going on my own so I dragged Tessa and some others along with me. I think he felt the same as he came mob handed as well. Everyone stared at us as we had an awkward chat and quickly realised this was a no go, then had a much better time with our friends.

Franz started going out with Melanie, a friend of my brother's, a relationship I wasn't keen about. I thought Franz was much too old and staid for her. I also think I was a bit jealous. Melanie was my friend and I felt protective. Franz had just come back from being a roadie in Europe and had taken back his old room and got his dog back from whoever was looking after it — a bone of contention as Joe and Pam had gone travelling and the last thing Pam said was:

'If Franz comes back, can you please not let the dog come back? He chews everything and smells bad.'

At a house meeting to consider Franz moving back in, I felt duty bound to relay Pam's requests. They were disregarded though as we all loved the huge stupid Wuffel even though he did smell a bit.

Before Franz, Melanie was going out with some boy from the squats. I thought she could do better as he was a bit tatty. I had a fling with his friend who I thought was a better bet, even though we both knew it was a one or two night stand. When Franz came back he made a beeline for Melanie. She was pretty and young and seemed to like him. I had no idea why.

One embarrassing evening we were in my car and it was obvious to me that something was brewing between them, even though she was there with the boy. She made the boy sit in the front seat and said she wanted to chat with me, although we didn't talk much. I wondered if he thought I was with Franz and we were a cosy foursome.

When we got to the boy's house in the squats, he stared at Melanie as normally she would have got out of the car and stayed with him. However, she just stayed in the back seat with me and went a bit pink and stared straight ahead and didn't say anything. As we drove away his face was a picture of horrified incredulous hurt as it slowly dawned on him what was going on. He looked like he was going to cry.

'That was a bit mean,' I said. I could tell from her face that she felt bad and was on the verge of tears as well.

'I just couldn't face telling him,' she said.

Franz driving in the front looked like the cat that had got the cream, as well he might. I wasn't keen on the boy, but it was a nasty way to give him the elbow.

For whatever reason, she was keen on Franz. After a few weeks she moved in with him but we still kept up a close relationship and went out together now and then. His room had always looked like some kind of monk's cell — a mattress and some clothes and that was it. With his long hair and beard, he had a biblical air as well. However, after he came back from being a roadie and started up with Melanie, he seemed to have a minor epiphany. And a physical transformation. He shaved off the beard and cut his hair. It did make him look better although I still felt that he was too old for her. He had children somewhere and an aggrieved ex-wife. In fact, he had spent time in the nick for non-payment of alimony which might have also accounted for the sparseness of the room.

Having Melanie around gave him the kick up the backside he needed. One day walking past their room I heard all sorts of banging and crashing so I poked my head round to check it out and saw Franz standing in a cloud of dust. He had knocked

175

through the wall to the little unused room that was next to him. It was tiny, smaller than my kitchen, and had just been used for junk.

'I'm going to turn it into a kitchen,' he announced. 'It's a surprise for Mel. There's too many of us using the downstairs one.' I was surprised as actually only Franz, Melanie, Mik and his new woman were using it but I thought it was a step in the right direction.

'I was trained as a chef,' Franz said, wiping a sweaty brow. Even more surprises. I had no idea and had never seen him make more than toast.

Chapter Eighteen

My life was going well. Franz and Mel were on the first floor in front room. Joe and Pam returned from travelling and were in the back room on the same floor. Franz and Mel had their own kitchen, as did Johnny in the basement. So the old ground floor kitchen was just for Joe and Pam.

I didn't have a relationship but there were lots of flings and that suited me. I thought Joe and Pam were a bit boring and told myself that my years with Joe had been the best years and now I saw them as a tedious suburban couple. Pam had also started working in Adventure Play, working with traveller families. She let one of the older kids cut her hair.

'Trying to curry favour with the youth,' I said to Mel when we saw the result.

It was bloody dreadful, bits sticking up all over the place. Pam put on a brave face and said that it felt 'real' to her. She also sprained her foot and I helped her put a bandage around her ankle.

'It could be round your throat,' I thought, surprising myself and realising the bonhomie between us was not very deep.

Johnny had tinkered in the back living room, the one that was actually used. The front one was just for parties and sometimes a spare room. He had managed to find a stove and install it. We used wood from skips and gardens and when it was going it was toasty in there.

'I've got an idea,' Johnny said, looking at the flames with satisfaction.

'What's that?' I said, lounging on the mattress. Now that it was warm we all used the room much more. For me it meant relief from the fumes of the Calor gas heater in my little attic living room.

'I'm going to shove some potatoes in the tray. I think they'll cook while I'm at the pub. I'm meeting Tessa there.'

I considered this.

'Great idea, Johnny. I've got some as well, and some foil. Wait for me and I'll ask Mel and Franz if they want a last order's drink.'

'OK, if you've got any marge or butter bring that as well.'

'Yeah, and Johnny—'

'What?'

'If you're going to the pub, wipe the soot off your face.'

I skipped out as Johnny threw a cushion at me and missed.

That was the start of some great evenings. We would stoke up the fire, shove spuds in the ash tray and then go out, coming back to lovely, cooked potatoes. That year we also had our own Christmas day and all cooked different parts of a massive lunch that we ate sprawled around in the living room. It was the first year I hadn't spent the day with Mum and Adam. It felt very adult to have Christmas lunch with friends instead of family and such a rite of passage.

One night around Christmas I went out with Johnny, Tessa, Mel, and Joe. Pam was off visiting her folks in Edinburgh and Franz wasn't in.

We all came back after the pub, and I could sense that some big drinking and a late night was in the offing. Mel, Tessa,

Johnny, and Joe settled into the warm living room and started to drink some carry outs and eat baked potatoes. There was a wildness in the air. I wasn't feeling quite the ticket, had a cup of tea and escaped.

'Oh, come on, Deb. Don't be a party pooper,' Joe pleaded.

'I've had enough of you lot,' I said, laughing and staggering up the stairs.

After that I had some kind of flu and was out for the count for a few days. I staggered downstairs the first day to empty my wee bucket, phone someone at work, and get sick leave. The house was quiet, and I had a vague memory of hearing shouting and stamping the night before. I had had a fever and just thought it was part of my dreams.

'I bet everyone's still got dreadful hangovers,' I thought to myself. When I was better I would grab Mel and get a full debrief.

I paused outside her door and could hear someone moving around but didn't feel up to chatting, so I went back upstairs, got some water, and sank back into bed. There seemed to be more shouting and brief spells of quiet. The next day I felt weak and wobbly but managed to get to the kitchen and make some tea and toast. I felt slightly aggrieved that no one had checked on me.

'Some bloody friends,' I thought.

Looking out my window, the sky was grey and gloomy, so I just stayed snuggled in bed, making forays to the kitchen and the loo. I didn't bump into anyone and the house was still quiet. I tried to remember if anyone had said they were going away.

Finally, I felt well enough to get up so I had a wash in a bowl with hot water and felt a bit more human. I shoved some clean clothes on and pulled my bed covers back to air after the fever and sweats. I crept downstairs to use the loo and empty my bucket — I had been too ill to make the trip two floors down. I stopped outside Mel and Franz's room and heard sobs inside. I hovered there, unsure whether to knock. I didn't know if I could cope with a long discussion. As I stood shifting from leg to leg, Pam came out of their room. She paused and shot me a look of pure venom. I reeled back and thought, what the fuck was wrong with her?

'Do you know what's the matter with Mel?' I asked her.

She ignored me, barged past, and clattered down the stairs in the Doc Martins she had started wearing since she had been mixing with the proletariat. I felt a surge of irritation. I thought that I had been the bigger person and buried the hatchet 'and not in her head' as I kept reminding Tessa. There was no need to be so humpty. I could feel anger and tears rise. I followed Pam down to the kitchen where she started banging pans and crockery around. I leant against the doorframe and watched her. Whatever was the matter she wouldn't be able to hold it in going at that rate. The woman looked like she was about to explode.

'Do you know what's the matter with Mel?' I asked again.

She wheeled round to face me, a knife in her hand and green eyes blazing.

'Your fucking friend—' she hissed. I stood back a bit. Pam looked at the knife and put it down. She changed in an instant from blazing fury to icy control.

'Your friend,' she repeated in the same cool tone.

My energy was fast ebbing away.

'Pam, I've been ill for three days. I've been up in my bedroom, not that anyone came up to check on me, thanks. I heard some shouting and now I hear crying. What the fuck is going on? Just tell me before I pass out.'

She gave me a curt nod, convinced of my story.

'Your friend was having sexual intercourse with Joe and Franz found them at it,' she managed to spit out. She could see that I didn't know anything about this. I had often read about jaws dropping but never experienced it until now. She was obviously seething and also devastated. Part of me felt quite vindicated — it had happened to her, now she knew what it felt like.

She obviously didn't want to cry in front of me and with a barely suppressed sob she pushed past and rushed upstairs, slamming her door. I scuttled downstairs to see if Tessa was in visiting Johnny. I needed a fuller story.

As luck would have it, Tessa was there. Johnny was in the garden tinkering with his bird houses. Tessa was fed up with it as it involved lugging huge bird tables around shops to see if they would buy them. He hadn't had much success although they were beautifully made. I was glad that it was just us two in his basement for once. Johnny loathed anything he called 'gossip' and I called 'information', so it was best if he was out of the way.

The basement had a kitchen at the back that led to the garden. It was as basic as the other kitchens but much bigger and had a big farmhouse table in the middle that was usually covered in Johnny's various projects. He was so handy and creative. When we had parties, he was always rigging up lighting and brewing vats of home brew beer. I knew that what looked like piles of junk to me were precious objects to him and would be fashioned into something useful and inventive.

The room where Johnny lived was his bedroom and living room combined. It was quite dark although in the winter it had a comforting womb like quality. Tessa was sitting on the mattress sewing something under an old Anglepoise lamp. I flopped down next to her.

'Well, tell all. What the hell is going on upstairs?'

Tessa put down her handiwork and looked at the door, checking if Johnny was around.

'He's outside,' I said.

'Well,' she said, in a soft voice. 'It's actually really bad, really bad. That night we all went to the pub and then came back, I could tell something was going on. Mel and Joe were flirting and messing around. It was pretty obvious what was going to happen, especially as Pam was away for the night in Scotland and Franz had been out.'

'Where was he?'

'Oh God knows, having a drink with one of his Channel Island buddies. Where did you go to anyway?'

'I was ill. I had a horrible bug, a fever and everything! I could have done with a visit or two. I could hardly walk. I've only just got up and Pam shouted at me and told me the bare bones.'

Tessa looked at me with a professional air.

'You do look a bit pale,' she said, and laid a cool hand on my forehead.

'Oh, I'm OK now, thanks nurse. Too little too late. I needed that yesterday.'

'Anyway, they were downstairs in the front room stark naked when Franz came back. He didn't go in there at first. The light was off and as far as he knew Mel would be upstairs.'

'Blimey,' I said. Tessa was right, this was bad.

'It was awful. Franz came downstairs and asked if we knew where Mel was. Johnny had come down here and I had stayed up with the two of them. They were laughing and touching each other by then and I felt like a right gooseberry — you know.'

'Yes, I do.'

'Well, I'd just left Mel and Joe in the living room so I knew something was up and Franz must've seen my face because he rushed upstairs and switched the front light on and caught them at it.'

'Then what happened?'

'Well, he started crying and tried to have a punch at Joe, but it was a bit feeble. Once we separated them, he rushed back into his room and slammed the door. Mel was crying and Joe just shoved some clothes on and slunk back to his room. I think he knew what was coming for him. I stayed with Mel for a bit to calm her down. She knows what an idiot she's been.'

'Takes two to tango.'

'You always said that, didn't you?'

'Yes, and now it's come true. Sorry it was Mel though. What was he thinking?'

Of course there was still one part of the drama that I hadn't heard. We lit fags and sat smoking, then I remembered.

'Pam?' I said.

Tessa shook herself out of her reverie.

'Oh God yes, she came back the next evening and Franz must have been waiting for her because he nabbed her pronto and told her the whole story in graphic detail.'

'Oh Christ.'

'Yes, and then she disappeared into her room and started screaming at Joe then ran out and went into Mel's room. She was in bed, and Pam started kicking her with the DMs.'

'Oh my God!'

'Yes, and then Franz and Joe had to pull her off Mel. We both went up as it sounded like someone was being killed. Pam was spitting feathers and shouting and swearing at Mel — as though it was all her fault! Franz was sticking up for Mel and saying that Joe had talked her into it and that she's easily led and that he got her drunk.'

'Oh, for heaven's sake, that's ridiculous as well!'

'Mel's just been crying all the time now. Joe's had to sleep in the front room.'

'Back at the scene of the crime,' I said and we both sniggered then looked at each other guiltily.

'I did hear her crying in there,' I said.

We both looked at each other again and then I got up reluctantly.

'I'll go and see how she is,' I said and went up and knocked on the door.

I heard a little, 'Yes?' and found Mel alone, smoking, tear-stained and exhausted, still in bed. I made her some tea and opened a packet of biscuits.

'You poor thing,' I said. 'I know what happened.' She started crying again and I patted her shoulder. 'You're a twit, you know.'

'I know, I know,' she wailed. 'I shouldn't have done it. I was drunk and he was being so nice to me. I was flattered. It all just got out of hand.'

'Well, he shouldn't have done it either. It's not your fault and don't blame yourself,' I said. 'Anyway, what about Franz?' Secretly, I hoped they might split up.

'Oh, he was really upset of course but he understands and he wants us to stay together.'

I bet he does, I thought. She's the best thing that's happened to him in a long time and he won't give her up without a fight.

'Where is he now?' I said.

'He's out getting food and fags. He's going to make me an omelette.'

184

I heard the big front door open and jumped up.

'Well, I'll leave you two together.'

She looked up at me with alarm, her eyes spilling with tears.

'It's a right old mess, isn't it?' she said.

After that no one talked much about IT as I thought of the night. Things were never the same in the house and I was sad about it. Joe skulked about a bit and wouldn't meet my eyes when I passed him in the hallways. He was making dinner one night in the downstairs kitchen and I popped in after work and had a chat with him. We both smoked while he looked at the sauce bubbling on the stove.

'You know,' he said looking up at the ceiling as if he could be overheard. 'If it had been Pam walking in on us instead of Franz, I don't think I would be alive now.'

'You're right there, pal.'

He handed me a plate of pasta and sauce which I ate standing up, expecting Pam to appear any minute. I don't know why I felt guilty. It had nothing to do with me.

Pam had a defiant air for a while and Franz and Mel looked downtrodden and low but there were no more rows. The cosy nights round the fire eating potatoes and drinking carry outs stopped and no one used the living room downstairs anymore. We all seemed to retreat into our own spaces and there was an air of tension in the house. I mainly socialized outside my circle of housemates now. They were all in couples and trying to work stuff out and I was single and working full-time. Our daily rhythms and habits were all very different. I was hanging out with the playground staff and people from the squats. There was always a party or a pub expedition and the new world of going to clubs as well.

An independent cinema had opened in Brixton in the late 70s called The Little Bit Ritzy with cheap all-night showings of cult and alternative films like *The Rocky Horror Show* and *Eraserhead*. I had recently discovered it — very different from the Odeons and ABC of my childhood and eschewed things like Kia Ora and popcorn in favour of carrot cake and flapjacks. It was like a squat equivalent of a cinema; a bit tatty and loose about what you could and couldn't do. The people were young and arty and it quickly became a home from home. We would often go after the pub and I would watch the first film then drift off and have the odd, strange dream full of images from the second film before waking up, stiff and cold. In the early hours with dawn breaking, we would buy Jamaican patties from the van outside and get the first bus home, our fingers and bellies warm from the spicy pastry fillings.

Another regular outing was to a home hairdresser in a squat in Railton Road, the front line. I had never bothered with hairdressers. I associated them with my mum and the times I had to sit for hours with curlers under a hot dryer with nothing but old copies of *Readers Digest* to thumb through. I always emerged with big bouncy curls that I hated.

Since then, I cut my own hair or got Joe to do it. He pierced my ear as well with an ice cube and a cork and a needle. It worked quite well. Tessa had a perm. She was going for a 'coupe sauvage', very in vogue, but they set her hair on big rollers and she got the inevitable big bouncy curls. She came round crying with a hat on. I pulled it off and stuck her head under the tap in the little sink in our room. She emerged with the small corkscrew curls that she was aiming for. I was inspired and tried a home perm. It went quite well. When my mum saw me, she said, 'You look just like Barbara Streisand.' High praise indeed.

The Railton Road squat was occupied by a crowd of gay men who co-existed happily with the local community and during the riots were at the barricades on the front line, chucking bricks with the best of them. Getting my hair cut was exciting and as far removed from a normal hairdresser as it could be. For a start, the house was always full of people.

'It's a knocking shop,' explained Conor, the hairdresser. 'If boys don't have a room, they come here. We feel it's a public service.' There did seem to be trails of slightly sheepish men coming up and down the stairs at all times of the day and night.

Secondly, there was no mirror in the room, so I was never quite sure what was being done until it was finished. 'Ta-da' Conor would say and show me his handiwork in a small hand mirror.

The first time I went I was feeling adventurous and fed up with the traditional long hair with fringe that I had had since my teens. With my foray into new music and abandonment of the hippy look, I had inched the length up, but it still wasn't anything very interesting.

Conor raised an eyebrow as I settled into the chair and put a grubby towel round me and sprayed my crop with water.

'Oh, just do whatever,' I said.

'Shall I dye it as well?'

I paused to think.

'It'll take a while,' he said.

I had the whole day and Conor had a minion who was making tea, so I threw caution to the winds.

'Oh go on then,' I said.

'I'll have to go quite short to get rid of this perm. Is that OK?'

I nodded, speechless. It felt like the end of an era.

187

When he was finished, all that I knew was that everything felt light and I smelt of bleach. There seemed to be a lot of hair on the floor and I felt like Jo March in *Little Women*. I paid and squinted in the hand mirror and spent the whole journey home trying to see my reflection in the bus and shop windows. I couldn't see very clearly. I thought one or two people gave me a bit of a look, but I wasn't sure.

I got home and clattered down the stairs to see if Tessa was in.

'Oh, my good God,' she said. 'Come into the light in the kitchen.'

I stood by the back door as she held a mirror up for me. My hair was in a pixie crop with the fringe and back bits coloured a bright blue.

Tessa grinned.

'Do you like it?' I said, nervously.

'I LOVE it,' she said, her curls bobbing about as she nodded.

'Wow,' Johnny said as he came in to see what all the noise was about. I was pleased. He was the type of man who never noticed what people were wearing or how they looked.

I got good reactions from everyone in the house. Pam grunted and raised her eyebrows. She had never really recovered from the Mel incident or the haircut she let the traveler boys do to her. I hoped she never asked them to dye her hair. The damage they could do with a packet of bleach would be incredible.

I was desperate to show my mum my hair. She was normally up for anything new or in fashion. I was hoping for the same sort of comment I got with the perm. I wasn't sure that Streisand ever had blue hair though. I bumped into her in Westow Street. She was up from Brighton visiting my aunty Jean and on her way to The Queen's Arms. I called out and she clearly saw me then crossed the street. I was mortified and crossed over and ran after her to demand an explanation.

'What do you think you're doing ignoring me?'

'You look like a budgie,' she spat out. 'I don't want people to see us together.'

I was hurt although I could see the truth in what she said, and it did turn me against the blue a little.

Chapter Nineteen

After the recent schism, the house needed some parties to liven it up and bring us more fully together as a household. We had two events in succession, both themed. One was a 'bad taste' party where everyone wore the worse things they could find. Jumbles were a great source of inspiration and cheap. I found a blue bri-nylon dress and attached a plastic Babycham Bambi to the front. Lots of people wore flares, beads, and crimpelene, Margot from *The Good Life* inspired outfits.

We played lots of bubblegum pop — Middle of the Road, Abba, Kenny Rogers, Bread, The Carpenters — anything we could get hold of. I liked some of it but would never say. It was a roaring success. On the back of this we had another, more elaborate Hollywood-themed party. Lou had recently started attending a YTS (youth training scheme) theatre project called Spring Theatre Group at an old Salvation hall in Crystal Palace. They mainly lounged around and pretended to be sad, happy, alarmed, angry, etc. However, she introduced me and Tessa to the group and we all got on well. One couple had a sideline as DJs at a club night in Gossips in Soho playing jive and bebop. We asked them to DJ at our Hollywood party, which they were pleased to.

We built a bar that Joe lounged behind looking dapper in a white scarf and black jacket with a black false tache and his hair slicked back. I had a skirt I made myself of net and a black top with long gloves. The place was all spruced up and we set out little tables to give it a nightclub feel. Johnny even rigged up lights to go on each table.

'Oh, for God's sake, Franz, you're messing the place up,' I said.

'I'm just rolling a spliff ready.'

'Yes, but you're not dressed and getting tobacco everywhere.'

He went upstairs. I don't think he really got the theme idea. For him a party was some Pink Floyd, plenty of spliff, and lots of people sitting around on the floor.

We did have drugs at the party. Joe made a punch of mushrooms and tequila, getting those who drank it completely wasted. A little bloke came up from the squats who I wasn't that keen on.

'Have you seen what Maggot is wearing?' Tessa said.

'Why Maggot?'

'He reminds me of something you might dig up from the ground — uuugh!'

I went over to the bar where he was standing and saw that for some reason his nod to dressing up was large false ears. He bought a bloke with him, Paul, who lived in Worthing and wore a suit and tie.

'Hello, darling,' he said. He was a great dancer and loved Tamla Motown so we got on well and he stayed the night with me.

'I'm married,' he told me straight away.

'OK, that's fine.'

It actually suited me. I didn't want a full-time relationship and seeing him every now and then was fine by me. We started an on-off type of thing where he would come to see me once in a while. We spent New Year's Eve together in a pub in East Croydon. Eventually he left his wife and small son and that was when I ended it. I was in a panic and realised he wasn't for me. He was different from any of the men I had been out with, which attracted me, but there was a criminal streak in him. He had been in prison and was possessive of me. He would 'have words' if anyone spoke to me when he was there. The novelty wore off quickly and we had nothing in common except Tamla. He was also keen that I got pregnant and wanted me to have a girl which, he assured me, he could guarantee.

I had a succession of short relationships as well as party encounters. There was Chris who Tessa named 'Winnie the Poo'. I had no idea why. We briefly worked together at The Queen's Arms and then he split up with his girlfriend about the same time I split with Joe. We got together out of loneliness and spite towards our ex-partners. He was a lovely man, but I wasn't the girl for him. After a while he made that clear and got back together with his ex. I couldn't see the attraction to her myself but he spoke of her in glowing terms.

I met another guy in a pub who was interesting. He was Jewish and left wing and we had some nice times together. I think he was initially intrigued by my background and lifestyle. He gave me the elbow as well and in return I went round to his flat in Stockwell late one night when he was in bed, and I knew he went to bed early. The flat was dark and then I heard the intercom crackle.

'What is it?' he said through the door as I leant on the bell trying to stifle laughter with Tessa. I was a bit drunk.

'It's Deb. I've got a pair of your shorts.'

He grumpily took them without a word.

The next morning the doorbell rang at Gatestone. It was the main one and not the drug dealing one, the two little wires at the bottom of the doorframe that you only knew about if you were a friend. I had never shown him that. No one else answered so I threw open my window and shouted, 'Who is it?'

He was there in the pavement smiling up at me, the bastard.

'It's me. I've got something of yours.'

I scowled at him. Touché.

'Just leave it on the porch,' I said. I wasn't going to give him the satisfaction of going downstairs.

'Are you sure? I wouldn't want it to get nicked.'

I didn't dignify that with an answer but shut the window and never saw him again.

After him there was Neil, the younger brother of a woman I worked with at the zoo. He had just moved down from Newcastle. He was sweet, a little younger, and quite open-mouthed at everything that was going on. We had a chat at The Queen's Arms and I asked if he wanted to come back to the house. He said that he was planning to ask me out on a date. I was so touched by this. It wasn't something that often (ever) happened to me and seemed so old-fashioned and quaint. I let him stay the night, in a chaste manner, but the next day it wasn't so chaste. He confided that I was his first sexual experience.

Although we didn't have much in common, our bubble of mutual charm, novelty and delight buoyed us along for a while. Occasionally we went to the pictures and the pub but spent most of the time in my place. His sister met up with us in the pub and seemed bewildered by our fledgling relationship but happy to support it. Neil was supposed to be staying with them but was never there.

'We must have you two over for dinner one day,' she said. I was quite happy to go along with this and try out the role of girlfriend for size, but Neil got cold feet.

'It's all happened too quickly,' he said a few weeks after we had met. 'I don't think I can carry on. I'm trying to find a job and my own place, and I think I just need to do that for a while.'

I was disappointed but knew I would always have an important place in his history. Tessa was relieved to see him go.

'What do you see in him? He's a beanpole with specs and a quiff,' she said.

I shrugged and said, 'I like the myopic way he looks at me.'

'It's just that he's shortsighted.'

In between these small relationships were even smaller ones. Men I bought back from the pub whose names I struggled to remember. That ended one night when I frightened myself by wondering if the perfectly harmless guy in my bed could be an axe murderer. After that I made sure I knew a bit about them and had some kind of connection first.

I went out for a drink with a friend from work. I had been promoted over him and he always resented it. After a few pints I was working up to lunging at him when he said to me frankly, 'I'm not going to sleep with you.'

Probably just as well, though I was a little hurt and embarrassed.

'I thought you might be the one,' he said. 'But then I realised you weren't.'

We got on OK at work and he confided that he was just looking.

'For someone pretty who likes me.'

Cheers for that, mate, I thought.

When Mik split up with Annie, he caused a bit of a nuisance of himself. She moved to a bedsit off South Norwood Hill and he used to go round there and shout and make an idiot of himself. He was such a mild-mannered bloke normally. She was now going out with a Scottish biker boy from the squats and finally Mik moved on. He found a lovely woman from Mauritius but she left him after a while.

He spent a lot of time round Gatestone and seemed to be just sleeping on people's floors. The breakup with Annie seemed to cause some kind of freak-out. He often talked about his time at Eversley with me and Joe like those were his glory years.

One night I woke up feeling that something wasn't right and found him halfway in my bed.

'What are you doing?' I hissed as he settled himself next to me. It wasn't a big bed, and I could feel his bony body next to mine.

'I have to be with someone tonight,' he said as though that explained everything. I could sense his desperation, but it wasn't enough to enable me to have sex with him. I was stone cold sober, I'd known him too long, and had no feelings for him other than a lukewarm friendship.

'Get out,' I said.

He made no attempt to move but just carried on talking as though I hadn't spoken.

'I've thought it all through carefully,' he said. 'I'm just not doing very well at the moment, and I think the best thing would be to kill myself.'

I was still half asleep and this episode had a strange dreamlike quality, as though I could blink and it would all be gone.

'Well, I'm very sorry,' I said cautiously.

He turned to me and said, 'Please can you just hold me. I'm begging you. I just feel so awful.'

Here was a soul in pain I reasoned to myself. It wouldn't cost me anything and might help. I slowly put my arms around him, but he saw that as a green light and started feeling me up and down.

'No, Mik, I told you no!'

'As you wish,' he said and nestled into me.

I lay there rigid until dawn broke and I could hear his breathing slow down. As soon as I thought it was safe, I took a blanket off the bed and crept into my living room to sleep.

When I woke bleary eyed to go to work, he had gone. He never mentioned it to me again and acted as though none of it had happened. I told Tessa.

'I bet you shagged him,' she said gleefully.

'Ugh! I didn't!

She kept teasing me and now and then we would look at each other, say 'as you wish' and burst into giggles.

After that Mik seemed to rally. He went off to Hebden Bridge for a while, a kind of northern hippy paradise, and came back full of beans. He also got together with Patty. She worked in the dye works off Gipsy Hill and often had multi-coloured fingers from the dye. She was married and had a child who was about seven. She must've got fed up with her husband as she took up with Mik. She was tall and skinny with long hair in a bunch sprouting from the side of her head. She became a regular fixture at Gatestone and was lots of fun.

One day Tessa pulled me aside as soon as I came back from work. Her face told me that she had some red-hot news. We ran upstairs to my place.

'Spill the beans,' I said. 'But wait until I've made a cup of coffee and lit up a fag and put the heater on.'

We settled ourselves on my big floor cushions and she said, 'Joe was in the kitchen yesterday and I popped in for a chat. Do you know that him and Pam are going to start up a health food shop in Church Road?'

I waved that aside. I had heard this from Joe and it seemed like a great idea.

'I might be able to work there if it takes off,' she said.

It was great news but didn't explain the air of repressed excitement that she had and the cheeky grin on her face.

'He told me something else,' she said, smirking.

I could see that she wanted to drag this out for greatest effect but also knew she wouldn't be able to hold it in for long.

'Tell,' I said.

She leant forward for privacy and then blurted out in one stream, 'Mik and Patty had a foursome with Joe and Pam.'

I made a gulping sound. I had taken a sip of coffee and actually thought that I would choke for a minute. She hit me on the back until my paroxysm subsided.

'Thought you were a goner there and it would've been all my fault. Although strictly speaking not my fault but them four's fault.'

I seized her arm.

'I'm fine, never mind that. What else did he say?'

'Not a lot. I think he was embarrassed but wanted to tell me. You know how he is.'

'Well?'

197

'He just said they both came round the other afternoon. Only Joe and Pam were in so they sat in their room and had a couple of joints and then Mik just came out with it. He said that if they were up for it, they would like a foursome.'

'What the fuck did Pam say? I know that Joe's a slut!'

'That's what I asked him. You don't think of her as someone who would be into that kind of thing, and I would have thought she would run a mile after the Mel incident.'

'So, what did she say?'

'She said she'd be up for it as a one off,' Tessa said and drained her coffee cup, ground out her fag, and looked like she was getting up.

'I've got to go. I told Johnny I'd help him flog some more bird houses and he's waiting for me.'

'You can't just naff off like that!' I screamed. 'More details! Who did what with who?'

'Oh, he didn't say. I'm sure he would've given me all the details if I'd asked but frankly I didn't want to know.'

'Do you think he said, "as you wish"?'

We both laughed and then Tessa remembered her mission and left me chuckling for some time.

* * *

Saturday started with a trip to a jumble sale. We took a dark-haired hippy from Portugal with us. I wasn't sure how he came to be included and I don't think he was totally clear either. Lou said something about him helping out at The Peanut Factory. His English was limited, and he was tall and suntanned, and had a hint of Cat Stevens about him. We were all pleased to include him.

At the jumble sale, he sat at the back of the church hall with the refreshments while we all pitched in and rummaged. Occasionally I looked up to check on him. He had a managed to get a mug of tea and a pile of biscuits and was working his way through those as an elderly woman with a flowery pinny and a felt hat spoke to him in an animated fashion. She shook her finger to emphasise something while he beamed at her in a bewildered but enthusiastic response.

I edged nearer, swapping places with Tessa and dragging clothes out from the piles. I was impeded in my progress by finding a black velvet cloak with sequins. I shook it out and held it up. I thought it might be from the 1930s. Tessa looked crossly at me.

'I was just going to get that,' she said. I stuck my tongue out at her.

'Hard cheese; it wouldn't fit you anyway.' The only part of me that was smaller than Tessa were my shoulders.

I nudged her and jerked my chin at Mr Cat and his new friend.

'What's going on do you think?' I said and managed to tune out the other noises to hear the shrill tones of the woman.

'And another thing,' she was saying. 'Something, something, something decimalisation.'

'Oh no, poor bloke. We should get him out of here before there's a row,' I said.

'Oh, he looks OK. Five minutes more. Let's look at the bric-a-brac.'

One tea set and a big brown teapot later, we whisked him out and walked home. We stopped at the Polish bakery and bought some babka and bread. Santiago (we found out his name) entered into the spirit of things and bought a whole load of cakes. We had managed to impress upon him the fact that we were going to have tea and cakes at home.

'Let's have a posh afternoon tea party,' I said to Tessa.

Back at Gatestone, we tidied the rooms and put Santiago in the kitchen with Franz while we went to our own kitchens and made sandwiches with the edges cut off. I made cucumber and Tessa put together egg and cress. Mel filled some bridge rolls with grated cheese and we had all got cakes.

We laid it all out in the living room with the new tea set and an assortment of chipped mugs and cups. As usual Franz just sat in the kitchen and rolled joints. We put him on making tea duty and set out teabags and jugs of milk.

'I wish we had a cake stand,' I said to Tessa. She was inspired.

'Let's use your red table.'

I dragged it downstairs.

It was perfect, if a little oversized. We hoisted it on top of the big table and left Santiago in charge of laying everything out while we ran upstairs to get into our costumes. We had decided to add to the atmosphere by dressing in our approximation of Nippies, the traditional Lyon's tea rooms waitresses. We all wore black dresses and I had made little headbands by folding a doily and pinning it onto a strip of paper. Santiago was enchanted by the whole concept. He found the rest of the doilies and spread them around the room kissing his fingers at me when I twirled in my finery.

Just as we finished the doorbell rang and our friends started to troop in. I had some ideas about Santiago but these were quashed by Lou.

'Hands off, lady,' she hissed. 'I just left him with you temporarily but I'm back now.' She looped her hand through his arm and sat him down on the mattress, plonking a slice of cake in one of his hands and a mug of tea in the other. He seemed amenable.

It was a lovely afternoon. Everyone brought cakes, we played jazz, ate lots, and had the best time. Afternoon leaked into evening and tea was replaced by home brew, wine, and joints. Cakes became chips from the chippy and our paper lace headbands were squashed underfoot with fag ash. For a while it seemed like we were in the 1920s.

There was a memorable dinner party at Ryan's. He had been in a bad state. Him and his boyfriend, one of Adam's young mates, were selling themselves in Piccadilly working as rent boys for married businessmen. He had got into heroin in a big way and, unusually for a junkie, put on weight. He had a fire at his place and one of his dogs died. This was a turning point and he got clean, lost weight, got a new squat, and managed to sign on and get himself an income.

To celebrate this new life, he decided to have a dinner party and we had a long discussion about this as he knew I liked cooking.

'I want to have some classy food — you know, not just brown rice and sauce. I want this to be a really posh dinner party, people dressed up, napkins, the lot.'

'It'll be lovely. You going to have a bit of a clean up?' I asked looking at the empty dog food tins that littered his place.

'Oh yes, don't you worry. It'll be transformed!'

And indeed it was, or because it was dark and had some skillful lighting no one noticed if it wasn't. We had all dressed up in our own approximations of 'posh'. There were about twelve people there including Pam and Joe who were sat next to me. Ryan had written little seating labels and I didn't want to ruin them by moving.

When we had the first course and all was going well, Pam turned to me.

'You know in the zoo,' she began. 'Well, this sounds strange, but can you smell?' She sniffed the air and I followed suit.

'Billy goat,' we both said to each other and laughed as the idea was so bizarre.

But it wasn't. A little goat came into the room, jumped on the table (a rather fragile arrangement of wallpaper paste tables with a sheet draped on them) careered along and started eating. There was pandemonium, people screaming and running out of the room. Pam managed to grab the little critter by luring it with bread and then tucked it firmly under her arm.

'Where shall I put it, Ryan?' she asked. Poor man, he was scarlet with humiliation and weeping with his face in his hands. I patted his shoulder.

'Don't worry, mate, we'll get it all together. It's fine.'

'Oh that bloody goat,' he moaned. 'I ruin everything.'

I tried to reassure him and we managed to carry on and eat the other two courses but it was spoiled a bit. Mainly because of the smell and I wanted to laugh so much. I could tell as well that some people weren't used to livestock with their grub and were visibly shaken by the whole thing. The evening ended early with Ryan apologising over and over.

'Ryan, don't worry,' I said to him when I got my coat to leave. 'No one will ever forget this!'

Chapter Twenty

I had an upset stomach and slept downstairs in the living room to be nearer the loo. The symptoms were violent for a few days and then subsided to a constant pain. Everyone was nice to me and I got a family visit. My mother, Aunty, and Nana came to see me. Nana, wearing a mink coat, looked with dismay at the room. None of them had been to Gatestone Road. It wasn't the best introduction as the room was grimy and I looked pale and wan. I was suddenly aware of the dust and the bareness of my surroundings. Since we'd stopped using it the room had been neglected. There was just the mattress with my used teacup and the cheese on toast I'd ignored lying on the floor beside me. My mother sniffed. I knew it smelt as well. A stale damp smell overlaid with patchouli joss sticks.

'This is like where we lived in Streatham, isn't it? It's got those high ceilings,' Nana said. I appreciated her trying to be positive but the atmosphere was frigid.

They refused all offers of tea and left quickly.

'Chin up,' Mum said as they left.

After that visit I assumed that I would recover and get back to my usual life. The problem was that I didn't get better and soon the offers of help from my friends dried up as everyone went back to their lives and expected me to do the same. I felt that I should be getting better, and I went back to work. I wasn't eating properly as it hurt my stomach and I had little energy as a result. I went to the doctor.

'What are your dreams like?' he said.

'I don't know, sometimes I remember them and sometimes I don't.'

'Do you have any problems? Anything that's worrying you?'

'Yes, I can't eat without pain and I've got no energy.'

He wrote something in a squiggle on his pad and tore it off and gave it to me. I dutifully cashed the script in at the chemist and took the pills religiously.

They didn't help. I had even less energy and slept so much that I missed mealtimes. All I did was go to work and sleep. I had always been self-conscious about my weight. I wasn't as skinny as my friends and had tried various regimes to combat this. Now the weight just fell off. My days and nights got confused with all of the sleeping and in the small hours one morning I woke up and went to my wardrobe. In it was a black cocktail dress I had bought from a jumble sale. When I got it the stiff material had clung to me and I hadn't been able to wear it. I kept it for the mythical day when it would fit me. That day had come. I put it on and stared in the mirror. Now it just hung on me, shapeless. It looked awful and I felt so depressed.

'This is what it feels like to be thin,' I thought and went back to bed.

At work everyone noticed my lack of energy but didn't know how to tackle it. I knew they were covering for me, doing some of my tasks. I had no energy to lead the team, and I was aware of sidelong glances and conversations that stopped whenever I appeared. I often fell asleep on the sofa in the hut. The crunch came as I was asleep when a child had an accident on one of the structures. The parents asked to see the person in charge, and I had to be woken up while they stood there. I sat up looking disheveled and groggy.

'Don't tell me sleeping beauty is in charge,' one of them said clutching a wailing child by the hand. 'What kind of ramshackle place is this anyway? I've a good mind to make a complaint to the Council.' My deputy led them away making sympathetic noises, shooting concerned glances over their shoulder. I was mortified and worried about losing my job.

At home my flat was grimy and unloved. The cat tray was filthy and the fish in my fish tank had all died. I ignored the cat when I was ill and there were times when I didn't feed her. I had no energy to cook for myself and lived on a diet of grapes and soda water. This went on for weeks.

'Do you want to go out for a drink?' Tessa said.

'Sorry, I'm too tired. Maybe tomorrow, I'll see.'

'OK, I'll let you know when the Remipeds are playing.'

After a while Tessa stopped asking me out. This was my new normal: sleep, work, repeat. It was a lonely and painful existence. I felt isolated from my friends and in a dreadful fog. If the fog receded then there was pain.

I hadn't seen my family for a while and a birthday party was organised for my cousin at Joanna's, a new bistro in the Westow Street. I knew they wouldn't accept any excuses for nonattendance, so I had a long sleep after work then struggled into some clothes that hung limply on me. I looked at my face in the mirror. I was pale and gaunt.

'Put some slap on, girl,' I said to myself and layered on lipstick, mascara, and blusher. Now I looked like a gaunt clown. I tottered down to the bistro and tried to smile and join in the celebrations. I couldn't wait to leave and go home but my mother had different ideas.

'She's got leukemia,' she said to my auntie in the toilet, crying.

'No, she hasn't. Pull yourself together and we can sort this out.'

Not knowing any of this I was sitting slumped in the corner, longing for my bed.

'You're not that great are you, love?' my mum said. I nodded at her.

'Why don't we go to your auntie's and look after you a bit?'

I was so relieved that someone was going to look after me that tears poured down my face. We got a taxi to Tulse Hill and I went to bed while my mum and aunty had a council of war. The whole family was horrified at my skeletal frame and sense of lifelessness. Opinions were split between me being a heroin addict or having a life-threatening illness.

The result was that the next day my mother phoned me in sick 'for a while' and whisked me off to a private doctor for a consultation. He looked at my medication and then at my notes. He examined me behind a screen, pressed my stomach, looked into my eyes and throat — the usual.

'Are you depressed?' he said.

'I'm just depressed at not being well.'

'The medication you're on is a strong tranquilizer. We give it to people who have trouble sleeping.'

The scales fell from my eyes.

'That's why I'm sleeping all the time! I took them thinking they would make me better and they made me worse!'

He nodded and started writing a letter with a gold fountain pen.

'There's something not right with you though. You need tests. You can have these through the NHS, and I'll make you priority. Don't worry, we'll find out what it is. Your doctor thought you had an eating disorder and were depressed. I think it's more than that, especially after talking to you.'

'What might it be?' my mum said, her voice quavering.

'Well, it could just be colitis or an ulcer or just inflammation — diverticulitis. Worse case is something called Crohn's disease.'

None of this made any sense to us but we dutifully looked as though we understood.

Back at my auntie's flat I felt relieved and even managed to eat tomato soup and bread.

After a couple of days, we went to St Thomas's hospital and I had some horrible things done to me that involved drinking chalky stuff and having tubes up my bottom. We got the results.

'It's Crohn's disease,' the consultant said. I felt my hands start to sweat and my mother went pale.

'Oh my God, no!' she said. I felt it was a bit dramatic. I took a deep breath.

'OK, what do I have to do?' I said. The consultant looked relieved that I was calmer than my mother.

'I'll give you some steroids. You have to keep taking them and make sure you don't just stop. After those you'll have some other medication. You need to eat very bland foods. Just rest and recuperate, come back to me and we'll see how you are.'

He was so measured and steady that I instantly felt reassured. We went back to my auntie's and I had pasta and cheese and started taking the steroids. I had some worries as my stepfather took these and it made his face swell. Luckily, I had no side effects and started to feel better almost immediately. A combination of being looked after, medication, and knowledge.

Mum had the bright idea of staying with my godmother and her husband in Hastings so she could catch up and I could recuperate. She got in contact with Tessa and arranged for her to pack me a bag with essentials then we drove down to the south coast. It was a lovely break with sunshine and people I rarely saw. I felt so happy being on the mend and I felt my energy and appetite returning.

'Now you've lost all that weight don't put it back on again,' my mother said.

At work I had worn a little vest one day and a colleague had gasped in horror, 'Oh my God I can see every one of your bones.'

I knew I looked better with more weight whatever my mother thought.

When we got back to London, I decided to move back to my home that weekend despite my mother's concerns.

'Are you sure the water is safe to drink?' she said. 'I don't want you getting ill again because the place is dirty.'

I was concerned about my flat as I had left it in a terrible state. I told Tessa when I was returning. After Mum dropped me off, I pushed open the wooden door. The house was quiet. I hadn't expected a welcoming committee, but it would be nice if someone were around to hear my news. I shouldered my bag and sighed, taking the stairs slowly one at a time. I paused on the landing, reluctant to face my hovel. I walked up my green gloss wooden stairs with trepidation.

'Surprise!' Tessa said. My friends had got together and cleaned my place from top to bottom. They had emptied and refilled my fish tank with new fish and cleaned the cat tray. It was warm in my living room with the Calor gas heater on and the smell of coffee brewing. My bed had clean sheets on it. Everything was the exact opposite of my expectations. I couldn't stop smiling.

'We felt so bad,' Tessa said. 'We didn't notice how ill you were after a while. You just stayed up here and none of us thought to check on you. I was a terrible friend.'

I hugged her. I couldn't speak.

'I did go to the doctor and ask him about malnutrition as you had got so thin,' she added. 'But I just didn't know how sick you were. Your mum told me the whole story.'

'It's OK. How would you know? That stupid doctor giving me those pills, no wonder I was sleeping all the time.'

We sat on the floor pillows, and I looked around with satisfaction.

'I can't believe how great it looks. You've worked so hard.'

There were flowers in a vase and a full Calor gas bottle.

'We've put some supplies in the kitchen,' Tessa said. 'Milk, cheese, white bread, pasta, and rice. I've looked up what you should be eating and it's all easy food to cook.'

I was so grateful. Grateful and tired. This time though the tiredness felt like a good tired. A result of being active rather than the pills. I nestled into the pillows and Tessa took the hint.

'I'll leave you now, wee pal,' she said. 'When have you got to get back to work?'

'Not until next week.'

'Well, you have a good kip and I'll come up later and make you dinner.'

I didn't know how long this would last but it was lovely while it did. The anxiety and stress I had been feeling for so long rolled off me. My cat appeared and formed herself into a little ball next to my stomach, purring. Tessa crept out while I sank into oblivion. As I went under, I heard her say, 'There's a letter from the landlord but I'll tell you about that later. Nothing to worry about.'

209

Even if there was, I felt better able to deal with it. I could deal with anything with friends and family. That was my last thought before I fell asleep.

Chapter Twenty-One

The letter from the landlord was something to worry about. It told us that in line with our agreement, the housing society wanted Gatestone Road back and would offer us 'alternative' housing. I felt a fluttery panic in my chest as I leant over Mel's shoulder and read it. Memories of living in Peckham came back. This time I would be on my own.

'There's a bloke coming round Friday,' Mel said. 'He'll tell us what's on offer then.'

Friday morning we all sat in the downstairs room, one of the few times we had been together recently. It was ironic that moving out brought us closer. Franz had told Mik what was happening and he came round for the meeting too.

'Well, I lived here all that time,' he said.

My friend Beth coincidentally came round for a visit as well. She offered to leave but I said she might as well stay and we'd have a cup of tea afterwards.

The main doorbell, the stranger bell, rang. Joe answered it. He came into the room trailed by a small bloke with a suit on.

'I'm from the housing office and I'm here to take down a few details,' he said. He didn't look comfortable. He wouldn't sit down on a mattress and kept inching towards the door. He

211

took off his glasses, wiped them, and started reading from his notes.

'Firstly, how many units are you?'

We looked at him blankly. He cleared his throat.

'How many people living here?'

Everyone looked down at their feet. We all had a distrust of any kind of authority and were reluctant to tell him anything. He was getting exasperated.

'I need to know how many flats you're going to need.'

We all looked at each other. Finally, Joe spoke up.

'We're one flat,' he said, putting his hand on Pam's knee.

'I'm one flat,' Mik said.

'So am I,' Johnny said.

The rest of us looked at each other. I knew that Mel and Franz were splitting up and I didn't want to be on my own anywhere. Mel raised her eyebrows at me and I nodded. It was settled in that instant.

'We're one flat,' I said pointing at Mel. Franz looked ashen.

'So am I,' he said.

Surprisingly, Beth raised her hand. We all looked at her while the man was filling his forms. She winked at me.

'I'm a unit as well,' she said.

'So, that's that settled,' Joe said to the man. 'Would you like a cup of tea?'

I knew the official was probably wondering if the water was OK like my mother did. He looked horrified, collected himself, and shook his head.

'No, thank you. Now we've done that I would like to see the house.'

Joe took him on a tour, and we all looked at Beth.

'Jammy bugger,' I said to her.

'Why not?' Mel said. There was silence and then we all burst into laughter.

'He'll be wondering how we all fit in here,' Johnny said.

'Let him wonder,' Pam said. It was a moment of squatter solidarity, feuds forgotten.

A week later the official letter came. We gathered again to read it. I was itching to see it, but we made sure that Mik and Beth were there before we opened it. Pam did the honours, read it and laughed, pleased.

Johnny took the letter off Pam.

'May I?' he said. I grinned at him. He wasn't her biggest fan.

'St Aubyns Road,' he said and we all cheered.

The new flats were in a cul-de-sac just round the corner, off the main street, with old newspaper offices at the end that were squatted. I first met Joe and Jimmy when Tessa was living next door to their squat in a rent paying house share.

When Joe and I first got together, the SPG (Special Patrol Group) had raided the squat and burst into his bedroom looking through drawers and cupboards. We were in bed and Jimmy came in the room and asked them what they were looking for.

'Where's the arsenal?' they demanded.

'Up the Highbury,' he said. It didn't go down well.

I had what I thought I wanted — to share a flat with Mel. Now I wasn't completely sure. I was in the tender and early throes of a new relationship. We had met before the eviction; he wasn't part of the squat scene and it felt like it was going somewhere. We were even vaguely talking about moving in together — it felt promising.

'Fuck me. Back to where we started,' Joe said.

He looked over at me with a sideways glance. The 'we' meant him and me, not Pam. She snatched the letter out of his hands.

'Let me see, darling,' she said and pursed her lips.

Mel raised her eyebrows and I shrugged. I felt a moment of regret. If I had been brave enough to put myself down as a single unit then I could have had a flat to myself, and maybe moved my new boyfriend in. I caught Mel looking at me and knew she was thinking the same thing. It was done and I wouldn't want to see her out of a home. We would make it work and it would be great.

The flats were in an old house that had just been reconditioned, spanking new. We were allowed a viewing before our move. We all ran in and out of the units, awed by the shining kitchens, the gleaming bathrooms, the hot water. There was a tiny garden area off the basement flat at the back. Instantly it felt this was the unit that I wanted but would require some skilful negotiation. I nudged Mel.

'We've got cats,' I said as we walked around the basement flat. It was designed for one person and was the smallest unit but had its own front door.

'We can have the living room as a bedroom and use the hall as a living room,' I said.

'Yeees,' she said checking out the galley kitchen. The hall was wide enough for a sofa and a TV although it didn't have a window.

Gradually everyone came down to the basement flat to check it out.

'This can be ours,' I said, with an air of finality. 'We've got cats.' Franz leant against the door frame. I was worried that he'd leave a grubby mark on it — on my flat, I felt determined.

'I do have Wuffel,' he said.

'It's not big enough for a dog,' I said.

I could sense Pam was fuming but didn't have a convincing argument to counter with. She let out a loud snort and flounced out.

'I take it that's a yes,' I said. Joe followed her.

'We want the top flat,' he said over his shoulder. 'Less noise.'

Beth, the interloper, was pleased to get whatever she was offered. Franz bid for the ground floor as then he could get out with the dog. Mik had the flat next to him. Johnny had the first floor and Beth the second floor. It was all decided with little bloodshed.

We gathered in Gatestone again.

'Right,' Johnny said. 'This is how it goes.' He paced up and down the room and spoke with an unaccustomed air of authority. We sat in a row on the mattress and the floor and listened.

'I've got a mate with a van and we all chip in.'

Franz opened his mouth to interrupt.

'It'll be cheap, don't worry,' Johnny added. 'We keep loading and unloading until it's all gone and then we move everyone's stuff into their flats — Joe and Pam's first as it's on the top.'

'Yes, that's a good idea,' Pam said but Johnny cut her off.

'Only when everyone's stuff is in their flat and Gatestone is empty do we start sorting our own gear out.' He wagged his finger at me and Mel. 'I know you two, no sniding off and hanging spangly curtains up or anything — hard graft until it's done.'

I booked two days off work.

Moving to the new flat was momentous. In one way it was just another move in a long series of moves, but it was more than that. The people in the new house were the same. I was surrounded by Gatestone people, but we were now in our own separate units; separated by walls, doors, and more inclined to lead our different lives.

Mel and I flipped a coin for the choice of bedrooms and to my delight I got the bigger one. It was the room that was meant as a living room, had a bay window and light. Mel's room was at the back of the flat and was smaller and darker. She was disappointed at first but consoled herself by saying, 'It'll be quieter away from the road.'

For this flat I bought my first ever piece of furniture and had it delivered — a pine double bed for £50. It was so grown up. Mel tried it for size in the new place when it arrived.

'It seems miles off the floor,' she said, sprawling over the bed. It was on another new purchase — carpet. I had bought the cheapest cord I could find but paid carpet fitters to measure, deliver, and lay it. Pale green and pristine. We both lay down and rolled on it.

'Do you think you'll ever miss skips?' Mel sighed.

I sat up on my elbows and looked down at her, considering.

'I don't think so, there were a lot of things that had been weed on. This smells so clean.'

I lay face down and luxuriated in the slightly chemical notes of new carpet. Mel sat cross-legged and picked at a loose tuft.

'There were some bargains though, and the excitement of never knowing what was at the bottom,' Mel said.

I leant against a wall and looked around the room planning where my possessions would go.

'It's given me a bit of a taste,' I said. 'I might get a wardrobe next — secondhand, but from a shop.'

Mel threw the ball of fluff at me.

'Ooh, get you!' she laughed. 'Lady muck with her bought stuff, paying rent, with a steady boyfriend, and a permanent job in charge of people!'

When she put it like that I realised how different my life was from those first months in Farquhar and how many things had changed. I had all the things that Mel had said, almost accused me of, and I was happy with them. I liked being one of only two women senior playleaders in the GLC. I liked the prestige. I knew I would enjoy living in the flat. It was clean. There weren't any dank glory holes that needed to be covered with spray paint or an Indian throw, no smells that required perpetual burning of joss sticks. I was happy in my new relationship and excited to see where it would lead to, but I had no idea what the future would hold.

Since I moved into Farquhar Road eight years ago everything had changed: the way I looked, the music I listened to, my friends, my relationship, my work. It was all completely different. I had come through some amazing times but also sadness and heartache. I knew that anything I had now I had got the hard way. Ahead of me there would be more of the same, I was sure. I hauled myself to my feet.

'Give me a hand getting all my crap back in here?' I said to Mel, stretching out a hand. She grasped it and heaved herself up.

'Reckon some chocolate bikkies should be payment enough,' she said.

About the Author

I was born and bred in South London and moved to Brighton in 1986. I have worked since I was fifteen as a barmaid, cleaner, zookeeper, adventure play leader, youth worker, primary teacher, childcare and Ofsted inspector, trainer, and senior lecturer in education. My most rewarding teaching was with people who had left school at a young age and were now reclaiming their education. I have a BA and MA (Film Studies) from the Open University and also taught children's literature there. I have written and co-written six books on early years, mainly focusing on equalities, LGBT issues, leadership, and grief and loss in children's lives. The *Peanut Factory* is my debut memoir. I now live happily by the sea with my partner where I write, swim, and travel.

Twitter: @debredprice
Instagram: @debredprice

Acknowledgments

Thank you to Julianne for wanting to publish my story and to Sandi, Allie, Nikki, Lucy, Suzanna, and Lisa for giving me great advice and letting me share many drafts while I was writing. I also want to thank old friends for sharing their memories with me: Jim Meteyard, Danny Lubert, Jackie Rogers, Liz Nolan, Kerri Sharp, and Mark Steel. Thanks to Lizzie Barrington for her encouragement. Finally I want to thank Maria Jastrzebska for her endless support.

Deborah Price
27 February 2022

About Guts Publishing

 Established in May 2019, we are an independent publisher in London. The name came from the obvious—it takes guts to publish just about anything. We are the home to the freaks and misfits of the literary world.

We like uncomfortable topics. Our tagline: Ballsy books about life. Our thinking: the book market has enough ball-less books and we're happy to shake things up a bit.

The Peanut Factory (May 2022) is our seventh book.

Blade in the Shadow (Oct 2021) by Jillian Halket. A coming-of-age memoir about a young Scottish woman struggling with undiagnosed obsessive compulsive disorder.

Fish Town (Apr 2021) by John Gerard Fagan. A young man's bittersweet departure from Glasgow and the next seven years of his life in a remote fishing village in Japan.

Euphoric Recall (Oct 2020) by Aidan Martin. The true story of a Scottish working-class lad and his recovery from addiction and trauma.

Sending Nudes (Jan 2021) is a collection of fiction, nonfiction and poetry about the various reasons people send nudes.

Cyber Smut (Sept 2020) is a collection of fiction, nonfiction and poetry about the effects of technology on our lives, our sexuality and how we love.

Stories About Penises (Nov 2019) is a collection of fiction, nonfiction and poetry about, well, exactly what it sounds like. To quote a prominent Australian author, 'Quite possibly the best title of the year.' We think so too.

Our website: gutspublishing.com
Our email: gutspublishing@gmail.com

Thank you for reading and thank you for your support!

Lightning Source UK Ltd.
Milton Keynes UK
UKHW010622260522
403550UK00004B/85

9 781838 471941